Fifty-Two Sunday Dinners

Menu

Oysters on the Half Shell

Mangoes   Salted Nuts   Olives

Consommé Duchess—Imperial Sticks

Crab Meat in Timbale Cases

"Green" Goose Roasted—Potato and Nut Stuffing

Chantilly Apple Sauce

Onions au Gratin

Endive, Celery and Green Pepper Salad

Vanilla Ice Cream—Chocolate Sauce

Cocoanut Cubes—Chocolate Nut Cake

Fruit   Raisins   Nuts

Roquefort Cheese—Water Biscuit

Café Noir

OYSTERS ON THE HALF SHELL
3 dozen oysters.
2 lemons cut in quarters.

A Book of Recipes

Salt, pepper, Tobasco, horseradish and Tomato catsup.

PROCESS: If possible, have the little Blue Points. Open, loosen, and leave them on the lower shell. Fill soup plates with shaved ice and arrange shell on ice having the small end of shells point toward center of the plate. Wash lemons, cut in quarters, remove seeds and serve one-quarter in center of each plate. Garnish with sprays of parsley arranged between the shells. Pass remaining ingredients on a small silver tray, or a cocktail dressing may be made and served in a small glass dish and passed to each guest.

CONSOMMÉ DUCHESS

Consommé served with a meringue, prepared as follows: Beat the whites of eggs very stiff and drop by heaping tablespoonsful into milk heated to the scalding point in a shallow vessel (a dripping pan is the best), using care that milk does not scorch. Turn each spoonful, allowing it to cook, until it sets. Place one of these individual meringues on the top of each service of consommé, and sprinkle with finely chopped parsley. Serve with Imperial Sticks.

IMPERIAL STICKS

Cut stale bread in one-third inch slices, remove the crusts. Spread thinly with butter. Cut slices in one-third inch strips, put on a tin sheet and bake until a delicate brown in a hot oven. Pile "log cabin" fashion on a plate covered with a doily, or serve two sticks on plate by the side of cup in which soup is served.

CRAB MEAT IN TIMBALE CASES

8 Timbale cases.
2 cups crab meat.
3 tablespoons butter.
3 tablespoons flour.
Yolks 2 eggs.
1 tablespoon onion finely chopped.
Salt, pepper, paprika.
Few grains each cayenne, mustard and nutmeg.
2 cups hot thin cream.

PROCESS: Melt butter in a sauce pan, add onion and cook five minutes without browning, stirring constantly. Add flour and stir until well blended. Add hot cream gradually, continue stirring, add seasoning to taste. Remove from range and add egg yolks slightly beaten. Reheat crab meat in sauce (over hot water). Serve in Swedish Timbales.

SWEDISH TIMBALES

1 cup flour.
½ teaspoon salt.
1 teaspoon sugar.
1 egg.
⅔ cup milk.
1 tablespoon olive oil.

Process: Mix and sift flour, salt and sugar, add milk slowly, stirring constantly, add well beaten egg and olive oil. Mixture should be very smooth, strain and let stand over night. Heat a timbale iron in hot Cottolene, drain and dip iron into batter, (having batter in a small pitcher), place in hot Cottolene and fry until crisp and delicately browned. Remove from iron and invert on brown paper. These dainty cases are for all kinds of creamed mixtures. They are used instead of patty shells or croustades.

ROAST GOOSE
PREPARING THE GOOSE FOR THE OVEN

Singe, and remove all pin feathers. Before drawing the bird give it a thorough scrubbing with a brush, in a warm Fairy soap solution. This is very necessary for it cleans off all dirt that becomes mixed with the oily secretions, and opens and cleanses the pores that the oil may be more readily extracted. Draw and remove everything that can be taken out, then rinse thoroughly and wipe inside and out, with a clean crash towel; sprinkle the inside lightly with salt, pepper, and powdered sage. (The latter may be omitted.)

Stuff with the following mixture and truss as turkey.

POTATO AND NUT STUFFING
(For Roast Goose or Duck)

4 cups hot mashed potatoes.
2½ tablespoons finely chopped onion or chives.
1 cup English Walnut meats chopped moderately.
½ teaspoon paprika.
1¼ teaspoon salt.

½ cup cream.
2 tablespoons butter.
Yolks of 2 eggs.
1 teaspoon sweet herbs if the flavor is desired.

PROCESS: Mix the ingredients in the order given and fill the body of the goose.

ROASTING THE BIRD

After trussing, place the goose on a rack in a dripping pan, sprinkle with salt, cover the breast with thin slices of fat salt pork, and place in the oven. Cook three-quarters of an hour, basting often with the fat in the pan. Then remove pan from oven and drain off all the fat. Remove the slices of pork and sprinkle again with salt and dredge with flour and return to oven. When the flour is delicately browned, add one cup of boiling water and baste often; add more water when necessary. Sprinkle lightly with salt and again dredge with flour. Cook until tender, from one and one-half to three hours, according to the age of the bird. If you have a very young goose it is infinitely better to steam or braise it until tender, then dredge it with salt and flour and brown it richly in the oven. Serve on a bed of cress, garnish with Baked Snow or Jonathan apples.

CHANTILLY APPLE SAUCE (WITH HORSERADISH)

Pare, core and cut in quarters, five medium-sized Greenings. Cook with very little water; when quite dry, rub through a fine purée strainer. To the pulp add one-half cup granulated sugar, five tablespoons grated horseradish, then fold in an equal quantity of whipped cream. Serve at once with roast goose, ducks or goslings.

ONIONS AU GRATIN

Cook one quart of uniform-sized, silver-skinned onions in boiling salted water. When quite tender, drain and turn into a baking dish; cover with Cream Sauce (see Page 151), sprinkle the top with fine buttered cracker crumbs and finish cooking. Brown crumbs delicately.

ENDIVE, CELERY AND GREEN PEPPER SALAD

Select crisp, well-bleached heads of endive, separate the leaves, keeping the green leaves separate from the bleached; wash and dry. Dispose the leaves on individual plates of ample size. Arrange the green leaves first, then the bleached leaves until a nest has been formed; fill the centers with the hearts of celery cut in one-half inch pieces. Cut a slice from the stem end of crisp red and green peppers, remove the seeds and veins and cut in the thinnest shreds possible, using the shears. Strew these shreds over each portion and, just before serving, marinate each with French Dressing.

VANILLA ICE CREAM

¾ cup sugar.
$1/3$ cup water.
1 quart cream.
1½ tablespoons vanilla.

PROCESS: Make a syrup by boiling sugar and water three minutes. Cool slightly and add to cream, add vanilla and freeze in the usual way. Pack in a brick-shape mold. Bury in salt and ice, let stand several hours. Remove from mold to serving platter and pour around each portion Hot Chocolate Sauce.

HOT CHOCOLATE SAUCE

Melt two squares chocolate in a sauce-pan, add one cup sugar, one tablespoon butter and two-thirds cup boiling water. Simmer fifteen minutes. Cool slightly and add three-fourths teaspoon vanilla.

COCOANUT CUBES

Use recipe for Bride's Cake (see recipe on Page 175). Bake in a sheet. When cool cut in two-inch cubes and cover each cube with Boiled Frosting; sprinkle thickly with fresh grated cocoanut.

CHOCOLATE NUT CAKE

$1/3$ cup Cottolene.
2 cups sugar.
4 eggs.
1 cup milk.

2⅓ cups flour.
4 teaspoons baking powder.
¼ teaspoon salt.
2 squares chocolate melted.
¾ cup English walnut meats broken in pieces.
½ teaspoon vanilla.

PROCESS: Cream Cottolene, add gradually one cup sugar, stirring constantly. Beat egg yolks thick and light, add gradually remaining cup of sugar; combine mixtures. Add melted chocolate. Mix and sift flour, baking powder and salt; add to first mixture alternately with milk. Add nut meats and vanilla, then cut and fold in the whites of eggs beaten stiff. Turn into a well-greased tube pan and bake forty-five minutes in a moderate oven. Cool and spread with boiled frosting.

January
Second Sunday

Fifty-Two Sunday Dinners

#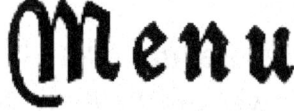

Consommé with Egg Balls

Celery　　Olives

Breaded Sea Bass—Sauce Tartare

Norwegian Potatoes　　Stewed Tomatoes

Cabbage Relish

Lemon Pie　　Cheese

Café Noir

CONSOMMÉ WITH EGG BALLS

To six cups of hot Consommé add egg balls, serving three or four in each portion.

EGG BALLS

1 hard cooked egg.
$1/_8$ teaspoon salt.
Few grains pepper.
Few drops onion juice.
1 teaspoon thick cream.
¼ teaspoon finely chopped parsley.

Process: Mash yolk, rub through a sieve, add finely chopped white, seasonings, parsley and cream. Moisten with some of the yolk of a raw egg

A Book of Recipes

until of the consistency to handle. Shape with the hands in tiny balls and poach two minutes in boiling water or a little consommé. Remove with skimmer. Serve at once.

BREADED SEA BASS

Remove the skin from a sea bass, bone and cut fillets in pieces for serving. Rub over with the cut side of a lemon, sprinkle with salt, pepper, dredge with flour. Dip in egg (diluted with two tablespoons cold water) then in fine cracker crumbs; repeat. Place in croquette basket and fry in deep, hot Cottolene. Drain, arrange on hot serving platter. Garnish with Norwegian Potatoes, parsley and slices of lemon. Serve Sauce Tartare in a sauce boat.

(For recipe for Sauce Tartare see page 84.)

NORWEGIAN POTATOES

Wash, scrub and pare six medium size potatoes. Cook in boiling salted water until tender. Drain, pass through ricer. Add six anchovies drained from the oil in bottle and cut in one-fourth inch pieces, one-half teaspoon finely chopped parsley, one-half teaspoon French mustard, salt if necessary, one-eighth teaspoon pepper, a few grains nutmeg, two tablespoons butter, and yolks two eggs slightly beaten. Beat thoroughly, place on range and cook slowly three minutes, stirring constantly. Remove from range, spread mixture on plate to cool, then mold like small eggs. Roll in crumbs, egg and crumbs. Arrange in croquette basket and fry a golden brown in deep, hot Cottolene.

STEWED TOMATOES

To one can of hot tomatoes add two-thirds cup toasted bread crumbs. Season with salt, few drops Tobasco sauce, two tablespoons sugar, and one-fourth cup butter. Heat to boiling point and turn into hot serving dish.

CABBAGE RELISH

Chop crisp, white cabbage very fine (there should be two cups). Chop one green pepper and one medium-sized Bermuda onion the same. Mix well and season with one teaspoon salt, one-eighth teaspoon black pepper, one teaspoon celery seed and three tablespoons sugar. Dilute one-fourth cup vinegar with two tablespoons cold water; add to relish. Chill and serve in crisp lettuce leaves.

LEMON PIE

¾ cup sugar.
1 cup boiling water.
2 tablespoons cornstarch.
2 tablespoons flour.
2 egg yolks slightly beaten.
4 tablespoons lemon juice.
Grated rind one lemon.
1 teaspoon butter.
Few grains salt.

PROCESS: Mix sugar, cornstarch, flour and salt, add boiling water gradually, stirring constantly. Cook over hot water until mixture thickens; continue stirring. Add lemon juice, rind, butter, and egg yolks. Line a pie pan with Rich Paste, wet edges, and lay around a rim of pastry one inch wide; flute edge. Cool mixture and turn in lined pan. Bake in a moderate oven until crust is well browned. Remove from oven, cool slightly, spread with meringue, return to oven to bake and brown meringue.

MERINGUE

Whites 2 eggs.
2 tablespoons powdered sugar.
¼ teaspoon lemon or orange extract.

PROCESS: Beat whites until stiff and dry; add sugar by the teaspoonful; continue beating. Add flavoring, drop by drop. Spread unevenly over pie and bake fifteen minutes in a slow oven; brown the last five minutes of baking.

Fifty-Two Sunday Dinners

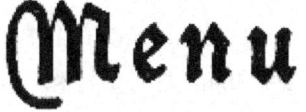

Noodle Soup

Boiled Beef—Horseradish Sauce

Baked Potatoes

Macaroni with Tomato Sauce

Chiffonade Salad

Steamed Cottage Pudding

Banana Sauce

Coffee   Tea

NOODLE SOUP
2 quarts Chicken Consommé.
1 teaspoon finely chopped parsley.
1 recipe noodles cut very fine (see below).

Process: Cook fowl same as for Boiled Fowl (do not tie in cheese cloth). Drain fowl from stock, and strain. When cold, remove fat, and clear. Reheat, add noodles, and simmer twenty minutes. Sprinkle with parsley and serve very hot.

NOODLES
1 egg.
½ teaspoon salt.

A Book of Recipes

Flour.
Few grains nutmeg.

Process: Beat egg slightly, add seasonings, add flour enough to make a stiff dough. Knead on a floured board until smooth and elastic. Roll out on a sheet as thin as paper, cover and let stand for half an hour. Roll loosely and cut the desired width, either in threads or ribbons, unroll and scatter over board; let lay half an hour. Cook in boiling, salted water fifteen minutes, drain and add to soup. Noodles may be cooked in Consommé twenty minutes but the soup will not be as clear as when noodles are cooked previously.

BOILED BEEF

Have five pounds of beef, cut from the face of the rump. Wipe meat, sprinkle with salt, pepper, and dredge with flour. Brown richly in an iron skillet in some of its own fat tried out, turning often. Remove to kettle and cover with boiling water. Add one tablespoon salt, one-half teaspoon peppercorns, a bit of bay leaf, one carrot sliced, one turnip sliced, and one-half onion sliced. Add two sprays each of parsley and thyme and one of marjoram. Cover and heat to boiling point. Skim when necessary. Reduce heat and simmer until meat is tender (four or five hours). Remove to serving platter. Strain stock and use for soup or sauces. Serve meat with hot Horseradish Sauce. (For recipe see page 51.)

MACARONI WITH TOMATO SAUCE

Cook one cup macaroni, broken in inch pieces, in boiling salted water twenty minutes. Drain, and pour over cold water to separate pieces. Mix with one and one-half cups Tomato Sauce. Add one-half cup grated cheese. Turn into a buttered baking dish, cover with buttered crumbs, bake twenty minutes in a hot oven.

TOMATO SAUCE

1 half can tomatoes.
$1/_8$ teaspoon soda.
1 teaspoon sugar.
6 peppercorns.

2 cloves.
Slice onion.
Bit of bay leaf.
½ teaspoon salt.
Few grains cayenne.
4 tablespoons butter.
3 tablespoons flour.
1 cup Brown Stock.

PROCESS: Heat tomatoes to boiling point; add soda and the seven ingredients following. Cook twenty minutes. Rub through a purée strainer, add stock. Brown butter in a sauce-pan, add flour and continue browning, stirring constantly. Add hot tomato mixture slowly, mix well, and pour over Macaroni.

CHIFFONADE SALAD

Cut the hearts of celery in one-inch pieces, cut pieces in straws to fill one cup. Remove the pulp from grape fruit, leaving each half-section in its original shape. There should be one cup. Peel and chill four medium-sized tomatoes (Southern or hot-house at this season), cut in slices. Cut the bleached leaves of Chicory in pieces for serving, arrange in nests on serving dish, and arrange other ingredients in separate mounds in the nests. Marinate with French Dressing, and garnish each with chopped parsley, green and red sweet peppers cut in thread-like strips, and sprays of pepper-grass or parsley. Pass Mayonnaise Dressing.

STEAMED COTTAGE PUDDING

3 tablespoons Cottolene.
1 cup sugar.
2 eggs.
1 cup milk.
2 cups flour.
3 teaspoons baking powder.
¼ teaspoon salt.

PROCESS: Cream Cottolene, add sugar gradually, stirring constantly, add yolks of eggs beaten very light. Mix and sift flour, baking powder and salt, add to first mixture alternately with milk; cut and fold in the stiffly beaten whites of eggs. Turn in a well-buttered tube mold, and steam one and one-half hours. Serve with Vanilla, Strawberry, or Banana Sauce.

BANANA SAUCE

1 cup water.
½ cup sugar.
Pulp 3 bananas.
3 tablespoons lemon juice.
2 eggs well beaten.
Few grains salt.
Few gratings lemon rind.

PROCESS: Make a syrup by boiling water and sugar ten minutes. Rub bananas through a sieve, add remaining ingredients and beat until well blended and light. Pour on hot syrup slowly, beating constantly. Serve hot. Pulp of peaches or apricots may be used in place of bananas.

January
Fourth Sunday

Fifty-Two Sunday Dinners

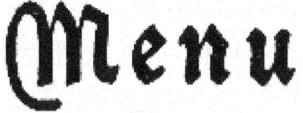

Corn Chowder

Crisp Soda Crackers

Ox Joints en Casserole

Boiled Rice   Parsnips Sautéd in Butter

Cheese and Pimento Salad

Ambrosia   Anise Wafers

Coffee

CORN CHOWDER
2 cups cooked corn cut from cob, or
1 can of corn.
1 cup salt pork cubes.
1 cup potatoes cut in cubes.
½ onion sliced.
3 cups water.
2 cups scalded milk.
1 tablespoon butter.
1 tablespoon flour.
$^2/_3$ cup cracker crumbs.
Salt, Pepper.

PROCESS: Cut salt pork in one-fourth inch cubes and try out in a frying pan; add onion, and cook until yellow. Pare and cut potatoes in one-half inch cubes, parboil five minutes. Add to onion, with corn and water; cover and cook twenty minutes or until potatoes are soft. Melt butter in a saucepan, add flour, stir to a smooth paste, pour some of the milk on slowly, stirring constantly. Combine mixtures; add crumbs and seasonings. Serve for dinner in cups or in small "nappies."

OX JOINTS EN CASSEROLE

Separate ox-tails at joints, parboil five minutes; then rinse thoroughly. Sprinkle with salt, pepper, and dredge with flour. Melt one-fourth cup butter in frying pan, add three slices onion and joints, sauté until joints are well browned. Remove joints and onion; to fat add one-fourth cup flour, brown slightly, stirring constantly. Add slowly two cups of Brown Stock, or water and a large can of tomatoes. Add one-half tablespoon salt and one-fourth teaspoon pepper. Turn into an earthen casserole, or Dutch oven, cover, place in oven and simmer slowly three to four hours. Add more moisture if necessary. Remove joints, strain liquor, return joints to liquor, add one cup each carrot and turnip cut in straws and parboiled in boiling, salted water ten minutes, and set in oven to complete cooking. Serve in Casserole or in a deep platter surrounded with a border of boiled rice.

BOILED RICE

Wash one cup of rice, drain and add slowly to three quarts boiling salted water so as not to stop water boiling. Boil rapidly until rice is tender (twenty to twenty-five minutes). Drain in a sieve, pour over cold water to separate kernels. Turn into double boiler, and cover with a crash towel; keep hot over hot water.

PARSNIPS SAUTÉD IN BUTTER

Wash parsnips, cover with boiling water, add salt to season. Cook until tender—thirty-five to fifty minutes. Drain and cover quickly with cold water; rub off skins with the hands. Cut in one-fourth inch slices, sprinkle with salt, pepper; dip in flour and sauté a golden brown in hot butter. Brown on one side, then turn and brown on the other.

CHEESE AND PIMENTO SALAD

Mix two cream cheeses with one-half cup finely chopped pimentos. (Drain pimentos from liquor in can, and dry them on crash towel.) Add one tablespoon finely chopped chives or onion, one-half teaspoon finely chopped parsley, season with salt and cayenne. Moisten with thick cream, and pack solidly in prepared green pepper-cups. Set aside in a cold place for several hours. With a sharp knife cut in thin slices crosswise. Arrange two slices on crisp lettuce leaves; serve with French Dressing.

AMBROSIA

6 sweet Florida oranges.
1 cocoanut grated.
4 plantains (red bananas).
$\frac{1}{3}$ cup fine table Sherry wine.
¼ cup lemon juice.
Bar sugar.

PROCESS: Peel the oranges, separate the sections, remove the tough membrane and seeds. Dispose a layer of orange pulp in bottom of shallow, glass, serving-dish, sprinkle with wine and lemon juice and sugar, strew with cocoanut and a layer of thinly sliced banana. Repeat until all ingredients are used, having a thick layer of cocoanut on top. The fruit should be piled in cone shape. Chill and serve with dainty cakes, macaroons, Anise wafers, etc.

ANISE SEED WAFERS

$\frac{1}{3}$ cup Cottolene.
1 cup granulated sugar.
3 eggs.
2 cups flour.
3 teaspoons anise seed.
¼ teaspoon nutmeg.
½ teaspoon salt.
Flour.

PROCESS: Cream Cottolene, add sugar gradually, add egg yolks, one at a time, beating constantly. Beat whites of eggs stiff, add to first mixture alternately with flour mixed and sifted with anise seed, nutmeg and salt.

Fifty-Two Sunday Dinners

#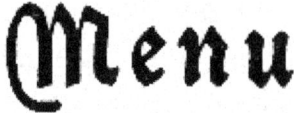

Oysters on the Half Shell

Consommé with Rice Balls

Braised Beef Tongue—Savory Sauce

Baked Potatoes   Bermuda Onions, Butter Sauce

Creamed Celery

Florida Salad

Yankee Plum Pudding—Vanilla Sauce

Coffee

OYSTERS ON THE HALF SHELL

(For recipe see Page 14.) Serve small cress or cucumber sandwiches with this course.

CONSOMMÉ WITH RICE BALLS

To six cups of hot Consommé, (for recipe see Page 149), add Rice Balls.

RICE BALLS

1 cup cold, cooked rice.
2 tablespoons flour.
1 teaspoon grated onion.
1 teaspoon finely chopped parsley.

A Book of Recipes

1 egg slightly beaten.
Salt, pepper, cayenne.

Process: Warm rice slightly and rub through a sieve, add flour, seasonings, and bind together with egg. Measure mixture by the teaspoonful. Roll in small balls. Poach until firm on outside in boiling salted water. Remove with skimmer and drop into clear, hot soup.

BRAISED BEEF TONGUE

Order a fresh tongue. Wash and put tongue in a kettle, cover with boiling water; cook slowly two to three hours. Remove tongue from water, peel off skin, and trim off roots. Place in Dutch oven or deep earthen dish, and surround with one-half cup each carrot, turnip, celery and onion, cut in half-inch dice, one green pepper (seeds and veins removed) cut in shreds, and two sprays parsley. Pour over one quart of Brown Sauce seasoned with one-half tablespoon Worcestershire sauce. (Stock in which tongue was cooked may be used for making sauce.) Cover closely and simmer slowly (do not allow sauce to boil) two hours or until tongue is tender. Serve on hot platter. Surround with sauce.

BAKED POTATOES

(For recipe see Page 140.)

BERMUDA ONIONS WITH BUTTER SAUCE

Peel the desired number of Bermuda onions. Cover with boiling water. Heat to boiling point, boil five minutes, drain; repeat. Then cover with boiling salted water, and cook until tender (from forty-five minutes to one hour). Drain well. Dot over with bits of butter, finely chopped parsley, and pepper. Serve hot.

CREAMED CELERY

Wash, scrape and cut celery in one-half inch pieces. Cook in boiling salted water until tender; drain. (There should be two cups.) Cut a slice from the stem end of one green or red pepper, remove the seeds and veins.

Parboil pepper eight minutes; drain and chop half the pepper fine. Add to celery, and reheat in one cup of White Sauce.

FLORIDA SALAD

Remove the peel from six large Florida Navel oranges. Separate the sections, and peel off the membrane, keeping the pulp in its original shape. Cut each section crosswise once. Dispose the orange cubes equally in nests of lettuce-heart leaves. Arrange the halves of English walnuts over these and marinate with French Dressing, using lemon and orange juice, also some of the fine orange pulp, in place of vinegar. Sprinkle with paprika.

YANKEE PLUM PUDDING

$2/3$ cup Cottolene.
1 cup N. O. molasses.
3 cups flour.
1½ teaspoons soda.
1 teaspoon cinnamon.
½ teaspoon cloves.
½ teaspoon nutmeg.
½ teaspoon salt.
1 cup sweet milk.
1 cup seeded shredded raisins.
1 cup English Walnut meats broken in pieces.

PROCESS: Cream Cottolene, add molasses; mix and sift flour, soda, spices and salt; add alternately with milk, reserving enough flour to dredge raisins and nut meats; mix well and turn in buttered molds. Steam three hours. Serve with Brandy or Vanilla Sauce. (For recipe Vanilla Sauce see Page 136.)

BOILED COFFEE

1 cup medium ground coffee.
White 1 egg.
6 cups boiling water.
1 cup cold water.

PROCESS: Scald a granite-ware coffeepot. Beat egg slightly and dilute with one-half cup cold water, add to coffee and mix thoroughly. Turn into coffeepot and add boiling water, stir well. Place on range; let boil five minutes. If not boiled sufficiently, coffee will not be clear; if boiled too long, the tannic acid will be extracted, causing serious gastric trouble. Stuff the spout of pot with soft paper to prevent the escape of aroma. Stir down, pour off one cup to clear the spout of grounds, return to pot. Add remaining half-cup cold water to complete the clearing process. Place pot on back of range for ten minutes, where coffee will not boil. Serve immediately. If coffee must be kept longer, drain from the grounds and keep just below boiling point.

Variety's the very spice of life,
That gives it all its flavor.

—

Cowper.

Fifty-Two Sunday Dinners

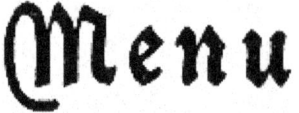

GRAPE-FRUIT COCKTAILS

TOMATO BOUILLON

LAKE TROUT BAKED IN PAPER BAG

SAUCE À L'ITALIENNE

FRENCH FRIED POTATOES   BRUSSELS SPROUTS

FRENCH ENDIVE—FRENCH DRESSING

EGGLESS RICE PUDDING—HARD SAUCE

COFFEE

GRAPE-FRUIT COCKTAIL

Select heavy grape-fruit (weight means more pulp than rind). Chill, cut in halves, and remove the sections of pulp, preserving the shape of sections if possible. Remove the skins from Malaga grapes, cut in halves lengthwise, remove seeds (there should be equal quantity of both grape-fruit pulp and prepared grapes). Reserve the juice. Chill fruit thoroughly, serve in tall stem glasses, add a little juice, sprinkle each with a tablespoon bar sugar, and just before serving pour over each portion one tablespoon Sloe Gin or "Sweet" Sherry Wine.

TOMATO BOUILLON

A Book of Recipes

To five cups of Standard Broth add one cup of thick tomato purée. Reheat and serve in bouillon cups.

STANDARD BROTH
(Beef, Veal, Lamb, Chicken or Game)

4 pounds meat.
1 pound marrow bone.
2½ quarts cold water.
½ teaspoon peppercorns.
4 cloves.
1 spray marjoram.
2 sprays thyme.
2 sprays parsley.
½ bay leaf.
¼ cup each diced carrot, onion, and celery.
½ tablespoon salt.

Process: Remove meat from bone and cut in inch cubes; brown richly one third of meat in some of the marrow taken from bone. Cover remainder of meat with cold water, let stand thirty minutes, then add browned meat and rinse the pan in which meat was browned with some of the water. Bring to boiling point and skim. Reduce heat and boil gently five hours; stock should be reduced to three pints. Add seasonings the last hour of cooking. Strain, cool, remove fat, and clear.

LAKE TROUT BAKED IN PAPER BAG

Clean a four-pound lake trout. Sprinkle inside with salt and pepper. Fill with stuffing (recipe next page); sew. Spread with soft butter, sprinkle with salt and pepper. Lay fish carefully in a well greased paper bag, add one-fourth cup white wine, one-half onion finely chopped, six fresh (or ten canned) mushrooms, cut in small pieces, and one-fourth cup water. Press air from bag, fold open end over three times, fold sides and corners close to fish, first moistening the bag on corners and edges; lay in a dripping-pan and place in a hot oven. When bag is browned evenly (not burned) reduce heat, and bake fish one hour. (Bag will brown in ten minutes.) Remove from bag to serving platter and pour contents of bag over fish. Serve with the following sauce:

SAUCE À L'ITALIENNE

2½ tablespoons butter.
2 tablespoons finely chopped onion.
2 tablespoons finely chopped carrot.
2 tablespoons finely chopped lean uncooked ham.
½ teaspoon peppercorns.
3 cloves.
2 sprays marjoram.
3 tablespoons flour.
1 cup Brown Stock.
1¼ cups white wine.
1 clove garlic.
2 teaspoons finely chopped parsley.

PROCESS: Brown butter in a sauce-pan, add onion, carrot, ham, peppercorns, cloves and marjoram, and cook five minutes. Add flour and stir until flour is well browned; add gradually stock and wine, strain, add garlic and simmer five minutes. Remove garlic and pour around Baked Lake Trout. Sprinkle with parsley.

STUFFING FOR FISH

1 cup cracker crumbs.
2 teaspoons finely chopped parsley.
1 tablespoon finely chopped pickles.
1 teaspoon salt.
1 teaspoon grated onion.
3 tablespoons butter.
¼ to ½ cup boiling water.

PROCESS: Melt butter in hot water; add remaining ingredients in the order given. Mix lightly with a fork.

BRUSSELS SPROUTS

Look over, remove wilted leaves from sprouts, cover with cold water, let soak one-half hour. Cook in boiling salted water until tender when pierced with a wooden skewer. Drain thoroughly, serve with melted butter, salt (if needed), and pepper, or reheat in thin Cream Sauce, allowing one cup Sauce for each pint of sprouts.

FRENCH ENDIVE

Remove the imperfect outer stalks from the desired number of heads of French Endive. If heads are large, cut them in halves lengthwise; if small, separate the stalks. Wash, drain and chill. Serve with French Dressing (see Page 83).

EGGLESS RICE PUDDING

4 cups milk.
$^2/_3$ cup rice.
$^1/_3$ cup molasses.
½ teaspoon cinnamon.
1 tablespoon butter.
½ cup seeded raisins.
Salt.

PROCESS: Wash rice; mix ingredients in the order given and pour into a buttered baking dish; bake three hours in a slow oven, stirring three times during first hour of cooking to prevent rice from settling. When stirring the last time, add butter. Serve with Hard Sauce. (For recipe see Page 161.)

February
Second Sunday

Fifty-Two Sunday Dinners

#

CHICKEN CONSOMMÉ WITH MACARONI RINGS AND PIMENTOS

BREAST OF LAMB STUFFED AND ROASTED

CURRANT JELLY SAUCE

SWEET POTATOES, SOUTHERN STYLE

BUTTERED STRING BEANS

CABBAGE SALAD

APPLE CAKE WITH LEMON SAUCE

BOILED COFFEE

CHICKEN CONSOMMÉ WITH MACARONI RINGS AND PIMENTOS

2 quarts Chicken Consommé.
½ cup cooked macaroni.
1 tablespoon pimentos.

PROCESS: Cook macaroni in boiling salted water until tender. Drain and pour over one cup cold water. With a sharp knife cut in thin rings. Drain pimentos from the liquor in can, dry on a crash towel. Cut in strips, then cut strips in small diamonds. Add both to Consommé, heat to boiling point and serve in cups.

BREAST OF LAMB STUFFED AND ROASTED

A Book of Recipes

Peel off the outer skin from a breast of lamb, remove bones, stuff, (see Page 36), shape in a compact roll and sew. Spread with salt pork fat, sprinkle with salt, pepper and dredge with flour. Sear the surface over quickly in hot salt pork fat, then place in the oven. Let cook one hour and a half, basting often with fat in pan. Serve with French Fried Sweet Potatoes and Currant Jelly Sauce. Garnish meat with sprays of fresh mint.

CURRANT JELLY SAUCE

To Brown Sauce (for recipe see Page 82) add one-half cup black or red currant jelly whipped with a fork, one teaspoon lemon juice and a few gratings of onion. Heat to boiling point, boil three minutes and serve in sauce boat. Onion may be omitted.

STUFFING FOR LAMB

2 cups soft bread crumbs.
¼ cup butter.
¼ cup hot water.
1 tablespoon poultry seasoning.
1 tablespoon finely chopped onion.
½ tablespoon finely chopped parsley.
Salt, Pepper.

PROCESS: Melt butter in hot water, add to bread crumbs, toss lightly with a fork. Add remaining ingredients in the order given. If desired moister, increase the quantity of hot water.

SWEET POTATOES, SOUTHERN STYLE

Peel cold, boiled sweet potatoes and cut lengthwise in slices one-half inch thick. Arrange in layers in a well-greased quart baking dish. Cover each layer generously with brown sugar and dots of butter, a sprinkle of salt and pepper. Continue until dish is full. Add one cup hot water and bake in hot oven until liquor is "syrupy" and potatoes are brown on top.

BUTTERED STRING BEANS

Remove the strings and cut beans diagonally in one-half inch pieces. Wash and cook in boiling water from one to three hours, adding salt the last half hour of cooking. Drain and reheat in White Sauce or dress with melted butter, pepper and more salt if needed. If canned beans are used (and they would be in some localities at this season of the year) turn them from the can into sauce-pan and reheat them in their own liquor. Drain and dress them with melted butter, salt, and pepper.

CABBAGE SALAD

Use only the center of a firm head of white cabbage. Shred it very fine and cover with ice water until crisp. Drain thoroughly and mix with one medium-sized, thinly sliced Spanish onion. Mix with either French or Cream Salad Dressing (for recipe see Page 105).

APPLE CAKE WITH LEMON SAUCE

2 cups flour.
½ teaspoon salt.
½ teaspoon soda.
1 teaspoon cream of tartar.
3 tablespoons Cottolene.
1 egg well beaten.
$7/8$ cup milk.
4 tart, fine flavored apples.
3 tablespoons granulated sugar.
¼ teaspoon cinnamon.

PROCESS: Mix and sift the dry ingredients in the order given; rub in Cottolene with tips of fingers; add beaten egg to milk and add slowly to first mixture stirring constantly, then beat until dough is smooth. Spread dough evenly in a shallow, square layer cake pan to the depth of one inch. Core, pare and cut apples in eighths, lay them in parallel rows on top of dough, pressing the sharp edge into the dough half the depth of apples. Sprinkle sugar and cinnamon over top. Bake in hot oven twenty-five to thirty minutes. Serve hot with butter as a luncheon dish, or as a dessert for dinner with Lemon Sauce.

LEMON SAUCE

2 teaspoons arrowroot.
1 cup sugar.

2 cups boiling water.
Grated rind and juice of 1 lemon.
1 tablespoon butter.
Few grains salt.

Process: Mix arrowroot, sugar and salt, pour on boiling water slowly, stirring constantly. Cook over hot water twenty minutes, stirring constantly the first five minutes, afterwards occasionally. Remove from range. Add lemon juice, rind, and butter in small bits. Beat well and serve hot.

February
Third Sunday

Fifty-Two Sunday Dinners

Scotch Potato Soup

Roast Shoulder of Pork

Spiced Apple Sauce

| Erin Potatoes | Boiled White Beans |

Celery Salad

| Squash Pie | Neufchatel Cheese |

Coffee

SCOTCH POTATO SOUP

1 bunch leeks or 2 cups onion.
1 head celery.
5 tablespoons butter.
1 quart milk.
3 cups potato cubes.
2 tablespoons flour.
½ tablespoon finely chopped parsley.
Salt, pepper.

PROCESS: Cut leeks and celery in thin slices crosswise and sauté in two tablespoons butter eight minutes (without browning), stirring constantly. Turn milk into double boiler, add leeks and celery; cover and cook until vegetables are tender (about forty-five minutes). Parboil potato cubes in boiling salted water ten minutes. Melt remaining butter in a sauce-pan, add flour, stir to a smooth paste, remove from range and pour on slowly some of the milk until mixture is of the consistency to pour. Combine mixtures, add seasonings, and cook in double boiler until potatoes are tender. Turn into hot soup tureen and sprinkle with parsley.

ROAST SHOULDER OF PORK

Have meat cut from "little pig." Wipe and follow directions for roasting Loin of Pork. (See Page 173.)

SPICED APPLE SAUCE

Wipe, pare and core six or eight tart apples. Place them in sauce-pan, add just enough water to prevent burning; add three or four cloves and half a dozen Cassia buds. Cook to a mush. Pass through a sieve; return to sauce-pan, add three-fourths cup sugar and cook five minutes, stirring constantly. Cool and serve.

ERIN POTATOES

Remove seeds and veins and parboil one mild green pepper eight minutes. Chop fine, add to Mashed Potatoes.

BOILED WHITE BEANS

Pick over and wash two cups white beans; cover with two quarts cold water and let soak overnight; drain and place them in a stew-pan, cover with two quarts cold water, add one small carrot cut in quarters, one medium-sized onion cut in half, two sprays parsley and one-quarter pound of lean salt pork, one-half tablespoon salt; cover and cook slowly until beans are tender (about two hours). Remove vegetables, drain beans. Chop the pork and mix with beans.

CELERY SALAD

Scrape and wash the tender hearts of crisp celery, cut in one-inch pieces; cut pieces in straws lengthwise; there should be two cups. Add one cup blanched and shredded almonds, mix well and marinate with French Dressing and let stand one hour. Drain and arrange in nests of heart lettuce leaves, sprinkle with the rings of Spanish onion thinly sliced (using the heart rings). Mask with Mayonnaise or with Boiled Salad Dressing.

Fifty-Two Sunday Dinners

#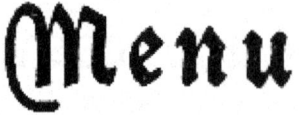

Tomato Soup

Roast Guinea Fowl—Giblet Sauce

Rhubarb Sauce

Potato Soufflés—Egg-Plant With Fine Herbs

Dressed Head Lettuce

Orange Ice—Chocolate Jumbles

Coffee

TOMATO SOUP

1 can tomatoes, or 1 quart tomatoes peeled and cut in pieces.
2 slices onion.
2 sprays parsley.
Bit of bay leaf.
4 cloves.
½ teaspoon peppercorns.
Few gratings nutmeg.
3 tablespoons butter.
2 tablespoons flour.
Salt, pepper, cayenne.

Process: Cook the first six ingredients together twenty minutes. Rub through a purée strainer, keep hot. Melt butter in a sauce-pan, add flour and

A Book of Recipes

stir to a smooth paste, let cook one minute; dilute with tomato mixture to the consistency to pour. Combine mixtures and season with salt, a few grains cayenne and a grating of nutmeg. Reheat and serve with crisp, toasted Saratoga Wafers.

ROAST GUINEA FOWL

Clean, singe, draw and truss in the same way as for roasting chicken. Stuff if desired. Sprinkle with salt and pepper. Lay very thin slices of fat salt pork over the breast, wings and legs. Place in a covered roasting pan, pour in one-half cup water, set in oven and roast from forty-five minutes to one hour (continue cooking if liked well done), turning so as to brown evenly. (When the roasting pan is used there need be no basting.) If roasted in an open dripping-pan, baste every ten to fifteen minutes. The flesh of this bird is dry and is therefore best cooked rare. Serve as roast chicken. Prepare sauce same as Giblet Sauce. (See Page 154.)

RHUBARB SAUCE

The young, tender stalks of rhubarb need only be washed, tops and root cut off, then cut in one-inch pieces (without peeling). Put in a sauce-pan, add just enough water to prevent burning. Cook slowly until soft. Add sugar to sweeten to taste, cook five minutes, cool and turn into serving dish.

POTATO SOUFFLÉS

Select six medium-sized, rather flat potatoes. Wash, pare and trim them square, then cut lengthwise in slices one-eighth of an inch thick (no thicker). Wash and dry them on a towel. Drop a few at a time into hot Cottolene (not smoking hot), fry them four minutes, turning them occasionally. Remove with skimmer to a croquette basket, let stand five minutes while the fat is heating. When hot enough to brown an inch cube of bread in forty seconds, place the basket containing potatoes into fat, shake constantly and fry two minutes. Drain on brown paper. Repeat process until all potatoes are used. Sprinkle with salt and dispose around roasted Guinea Fowl.

EGG-PLANT SAUTÉ (With Fine Herbs)

Pare a medium-sized egg-plant, cut in very thin slices, sprinkle with salt and pile in a colander. Cover with a plate and weights to press out the acrid juice; let stand two hours, sprinkle with pepper, dredge with flour, and sauté in hot butter until crisp and a golden brown. Mix together one-half teaspoon each finely chopped parsley and chives, one-fourth teaspoon very finely chopped chervil and sprinkle lightly over egg-plant as soon as crisp. Arrange on hot serving dish and serve at once.

DRESSED HEAD LETTUCE

Remove the outer green leaves from two medium-sized heads of crisp head lettuce. Wash carefully, without separating the leaves; drain dry in a wire basket or on towels. Cut heads in halves lengthwise and arrange in salad bowl. Set aside in a cool place, and, just before serving, pour over French Dressing. Serve at once.

ORANGE ICE

4 cups water.
2½ cups sugar.
2 cups orange juice.
½ cup lemon juice.
Rind of two oranges.

PROCESS: Pare the rind as thinly as possible from two oranges; add to water and sugar, and cook twenty minutes. Remove rind, add fruit juice, strain, cool and freeze. Serve in stem glasses.

CHOCOLATE JUMBLES

⅓ cup Cottolene.
1 cup sugar.
2 squares chocolate grated.
1 tablespoon milk or water.
2 eggs beaten thick and light.
2 teaspoons baking powder.
2 cups flour.
¼ teaspoon salt.
1 teaspoon vanilla.

PROCESS: Cream Cottolene, add sugar gradually, stirring constantly, add chocolate, milk and eggs. Mix and sift flour, baking powder and salt; add to first mixture. Add more flour if necessary. Dough should be soft. Toss on a floured board, roll out to one-half inch thickness, shape with a doughnut cutter, sprinkle with granulated sugar and bake ten to twelve minutes in a hot oven.

*What and how great the
virtue and the art
To live on little with a
cheerful heart.*

—

Pope.

Fifty-Two Sunday Dinners

Menu
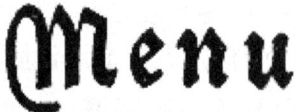

Spring Soup—Crusts

Breast of Veal Roasted—Brown Sauce

Spanish Rice   Mashed Parsnips

Pineapple Fritters

Red Cabbage, Celery and Onion Salad

Steamed Currant Pudding

Dried Apricot and Hard Sauce

Small Cups Coffee

SPRING SOUP
3 bunches chopped watercress.
1 bunch young onions.
3 tablespoons butter.
2 tablespoons flour.
½ cup thin cream.
Yolk 1 egg slightly beaten.
Salt, pepper.
Parsley finely chopped.

Process: Pick off the leaves of cress and chop fine. Cut onions in thin slices. Cook watercress and onions in butter five minutes (without browning), add flour and salt, stir until smooth, then pour milk on gradually, stirring constantly. Cook over hot water twenty minutes. Add beef extract, stir until dissolved; season with Worcestershire sauce and a few grains cayenne. Strain into hot soup tureen, add whipped cream and sprinkle with finely chopped parsley.

CRUSTS

Cut stale sandwich bread lengthwise in one-inch thick slices and remove crusts. Cut slices in bars one inch wide and six inches long. Bake in a hot oven until delicately browned. Turn them so that crusts may brown evenly on all sides. Serve hot and crisp.

BREAST OF VEAL ROASTED

Six pounds of veal cut from the breast. Wipe, and skewer meat into shape, sprinkle with salt, pepper, dredge with flour and cover top with thin slices of fat salt pork. Lay in a dripping pan and strew cubes of pork around meat. Place in a very hot oven for the first half hour, basting every ten minutes with fat in pan, then reduce heat and cook meat slowly until tender, allowing twenty minutes to pound; continue basting. The last half hour of cooking remove salt pork, dredge meat again with flour, and brown richly. Remove meat to hot serving platter, surround with Spanish Rice and prepare a Brown Sauce from some of the fat in pan. (See Page 82 for Brown Sauce.)

SPANISH RICE

Cover one cup of rice with cold water; heat to boiling point and boil two minutes. Drain in a strainer, rinse well with cold water and drain again. Cut four slices of bacon in shreds, crosswise, and cook until crisp. Remove bacon, add to rice. Cut one-half of a green or red pepper in shreds and cook in bacon fat until soft, then add pepper and bacon fat to rice. Cover with three cups of well-seasoned chicken broth, season well with salt, cover and let cook until rice has absorbed broth and is tender, then add one cup of thick tomato purée and two-thirds cup of grated cheese. Mix well with a fork and let heat through over boiling water. Serve with roast veal or breaded veal cutlets.

MASHED PARSNIPS

Wash and cook in boiling water, drain and plunge into cold water, when the skins may be easily rubbed off. Mash and rub through a sieve. Season with salt, pepper, butter and moisten with a little cream or milk. Reheat over hot water and serve.

PINEAPPLE FRITTERS

Drain sliced pineapple from the liquor in the can. Dry on a crash towel. Dip in batter and fry a golden brown in deep hot Cottolene. Drain on brown paper, sprinkle with powdered sugar and serve with some of the liquor from which it was drained. This may be slightly thickened with arrowroot, allowing one teaspoon arrowroot to each cup of liquor.

BATTER FOR FRITTERS

1 cup bread flour.
1 tablespoon sugar.
¼ teaspoon salt.
⅔ cup milk.
½ teaspoon melted Cottolene.
White one egg beaten stiff.

Process: Mix flour, sugar and salt. Add milk slowly, stirring constantly until batter is smooth; add Cottolene and white of egg. Batter must be smooth as cream.

RED CABBAGE, CELERY AND ONION SALAD

Select a small, solid head of red cabbage; remove the wilted leaves. Cut in quarters and cut out the tough stalk and the coarse ribs of the leaves. Cover with cold water and let soak until cabbage is crisp; drain, then shave in thin shreds, and mix with the hearts of two or three heads (according to their size) of crisp celery, cut in small pieces crosswise. Add one medium-sized Spanish onion, finely chopped, and dress with Boiled Salad Dressing. Serve in lettuce heart leaves or in nests of cress.

STEAM CURRANT PUDDING

3 tablespoons Cottolene.
½ cup sugar.
2½ cups flour.

3½ teaspoons baking powder.
½ teaspoon salt.
1 egg well beaten.
1 cup milk.
½ cup currants.

Process: Mix and sift the dry ingredients (reserving two tablespoons flour), rub in Cottolene with tips of fingers. Sprinkle two tablespoons flour over cleaned currants, add to first mixture; add milk gradually, beat well and turn into a buttered mold; cover and steam two hours. Serve with Dried Apricot and Hard Sauce.

DRIED APRICOT SAUCE

Wash and pick over dried apricots, soak over night in cold water to cover. Cook until soft and quite dry, in the water in which they were soaked. Rub through a sieve and sweeten to taste. Reheat, and drop a spoonful on each portion of pudding, place a small star of Hard Sauce in center and serve.

March
Second Sunday

Fifty-Two Sunday Dinners

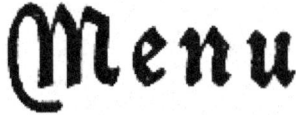

Chicken Stew with Dumplings

Onions in Cream   Stewed Corn

Watercress and Egg Salad

Rhubarb Pie   Cream Cheese

Coffee

STEWED CHICKEN

Dress, clean and cut up a chicken (a year old). Put in a stew-pan, cover with boiling water. Add one small onion sliced, two stalks celery cut in pieces, two sprays parsley and one-half teaspoon peppercorns. Cover and cook slowly until tender. Add one tablespoon salt the last hour of cooking. Remove chicken, strain liquor and remove some of the fat if necessary. Thicken the stock with two-thirds cup of flour diluted with sufficient cold water to pour readily. Return chicken to "gravy," heat to boiling point. Drop dumplings on top of chicken, cover stew-pan with a towel, replace the cover and steam dumplings twelve minutes. Arrange chicken on hot serving platter, surround with dumplings, sprinkle lightly with finely chopped parsley.

DUMPLINGS

2 cups flour.
4 teaspoons baking powder.
½ teaspoon salt.

A Book of Recipes

1 teaspoon Cottolene.
¾ cup milk.

PROCESS: Sift together twice, flour, baking powder and salt, rub in Cottolene with tips of fingers. Add milk gradually, mixing it in with a knife. Drop from tip of spoon on top of meat, an inch apart; cover closely and steam twelve minutes.

ONIONS WITH CREAM

Select silver-skin onions of a uniform size; peel and cover with boiling water, bring to boiling point, drain and repeat. Then cover with boiling water, season with salt and cook until onions are tender (from forty-five to sixty minutes). Drain and add one-half cup hot cream (to eight onions). Sprinkle with black pepper and serve.

STEWED DRIED CORN

Soak two cups dried sweet corn overnight, in cold water to cover. In the morning place on range and simmer slowly until corn is tender and water is absorbed, add more water if necessary. Add one-fourth cup butter, two teaspoons sugar, one-fourth cup cream or milk, salt and pepper. Be careful that corn does not scorch.

WATERCRESS AND EGG SALAD

Wash thoroughly, trim off roots, drain, and chill watercress. Arrange nests of the cress on individual salad plates. Cut four hard-cooked eggs in halves crosswise, in such a manner that tops of whites will be notched. Remove yolks, rub through a sieve, season with salt, pepper and moisten with Boiled Salad Dressing to the consistency to handle. Shape in balls the original size, dip in finely chopped parsley and replace in whites. Dispose one "cup" in each nest, and just before serving marinate with French Dressing.

RHUBARB PIE

2 cups rhubarb.
¾ cup sugar.
1 egg slightly beaten.

2 tablespoons flour.
Few grains salt.
Few grains nutmeg.

PROCESS: If rhubarb is young and tender it need not be peeled. Cut the stalks in half-inch pieces before measuring. Mix sugar, flour, egg, salt and nutmeg. Add to rhubarb, toss together until ingredients are well mixed. Turn into a pie pan lined with paste, heap rhubarb well in center, cover with a top crust and bake thirty-five minutes in a hot oven. (When rhubarb is older it may be scalded before using.)

March
Third Sunday

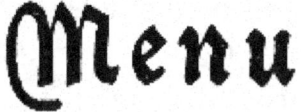

OYSTER COCKTAILS IN GRAPE FRUIT

PLANKED WHITEFISH

MASHED POTATOES

BUTTERED BEETS

ALABAMA SALAD

RAISIN PIE   EDAM CHEESE

BOILED COFFEE

OYSTER COCKTAIL IN GRAPE FRUIT

Prepare the grape fruit in the usual way. Chill; just before serving place five Blue Point oysters in the cavity made by removing the tough portions in each half grape fruit. Season with lemon juice, salt, paprika and one or two drops of Tobasco sauce. Serve on beds of shaved ice. Garnish with foliage.

PLANKED WHITEFISH

Clean and split a three-pound whitefish. Lay, skin side down, on a hot, well-greased oak plank (one and one-half inches thick and two or more inches longer and wider than the fish). Brush fish over with soft butter and sprinkle with salt and pepper. Surround fish with a border of coarse salt to prevent plank from burning. Bake twenty-five minutes in a hot oven, or place plank on broiler and broil twenty minutes under the gas flame. Remove to table covered with a sheet of brown paper, scrape off salt, wipe the edges of plank with a piece of cheese cloth wrung from hot water; spread fish with Maître d'Hôtel Butter; surround with a border made of hot mashed potato, passing it through pastry bag and rose tube. Garnish with sprays of parsley and sliced lemon. Serve immediately.

FRICASSEED TOMATOES

Select firm, not over-ripe tomatoes. Cut in halves crosswise. Sprinkle with salt, pepper and a grating of onion; dredge with flour and sauté in melted butter; brown first on cut side, then turn and finish cooking on the other. When soft, but not broken, pour over thin cream to almost cover. Let simmer until cream is slightly thickened. Remove to hot serving dish and pour cream around.

ALABAMA SALAD

Cut the hearts of celery in one-fourth inch pieces, there should be two cups. Add one cup of Alabama pecan nut meats broken in quarters and one cup white cabbage cut in very fine shreds. Moisten with Cream Dressing. Serve on a bed of cress.

CREAM DRESSING

3 hard cooked egg yolks.
1 teaspoon salt.
Few grains cayenne.
1 teaspoon mustard.
2 tablespoons vinegar.
Few drops onion juice or
1 teaspoon finely chopped chives.
1½ cups thick cream.

PROCESS: Mash and rub the egg yolks through a sieve, add seasonings (except cayenne), then vinegar and chives. Whip cream until stiff, and add a little at a time to first mixture, beating constantly. When all is used, sprinkle in a few grains cayenne or paprika.

RAISIN PIE

1½ cups seeded raisins cut in halves.
½ cup sugar.
2 tablespoons flour.
2 tablespoons butter.
Juice and grated rind 1 lemon.
1 cup water in which raisins were cooked.
Few grains salt.

Process: Cook raisins in boiling water to cover, until tender, drain, and mix with sugar, grated rind, flour and salt. Cool slightly. Turn into pie-pan lined with Plain Paste, dot over with butter and pour over water. Cover with top crust made of Rich Paste and bake thirty minutes in a moderate oven.

March
Fourth Sunday

#

CREAM OF LETTUCE

BAKED HAM—HOT HORSERADISH SAUCE

SWEET POTATO CROQUETTES—SPINACH WITH EGGS

GRAPE FRUIT SALAD

CHEESE BALLS

RHUBARB TART—CHEESE

AFTER DINNER COFFEE

BAKED HAM

Select a lean ham, weighing from twelve to fourteen pounds, cover with cold water or equal parts of water and sweet cider and let soak (skin side up) over night. Drain, scrape and trim off all objectionable parts about the knuckle. Cover flesh side with a dough made of flour and water. Place in a dripping pan, skin side down. Bake in a hot oven until dough is a dark brown; reduce heat and bake very slowly five hours. Ham enclosed in dough needs no basting. Remove dough, turn ham over and peel off the skin. Sprinkle ham with sugar, cover with grated bread crumbs and bake twenty to thirty minutes. Remove from oven and decorate with cloves; place a paper frill on knuckle, garnish with sprays of parsley and lemon cut in fancy shapes. Serve hot or cold.

HOT HORSERADISH SAUCE

¼ cup freshly grated horseradish.
¼ cup fine cracker crumbs.
1½ cups milk.
3 tablespoons butter.
½ teaspoon salt.
⅛ teaspoon pepper.
1 tablespoon vinegar.
2 tablespoons lemon juice.
½ tablespoon grated onion.

Process: Cook crumbs, horseradish and milk twenty minutes in double boiler. Add seasonings, vinegar and lemon juice slowly, stirring constantly. Add grated onion, reheat and serve.

SWEET POTATO CROQUETTES

2 cups hot riced sweet potatoes.
3 tablespoons butter.
½ teaspoon salt.
Few grains pepper.
½ cup chopped walnut meats.
1 egg well beaten.

Process: Mix ingredients in the order given. If mixture is too dry add hot milk. Mold in cork-shape croquettes, roll in crumbs, then in egg, again in crumbs, and fry in deep hot Cottolene. Drain on brown paper and arrange around Baked Ham.

GRAPE FRUIT SALAD

Cut three large grape fruit in halves crosswise, remove the pulp and keep in its original shape. Arrange in nests of white crisp lettuce heart leaves, dividing pulp in six portions. Strew one cup of English walnut meats, broken in fourths, over grape fruit. Marinate with French Dressing, but with less salt and using paprika in place of cayenne, and lemon and grape fruit juice in place of vinegar.

CHEESE BALLS

1½ cups grated cheese.
1 tablespoon flour.
$\frac{1}{3}$ teaspoon salt.
$\frac{1}{8}$ teaspoon mustard.
Few grains cayenne.
Whites 3 eggs beaten stiff.

PROCESS: Add flour and seasonings to cheese, fold in whites of eggs, shape in small balls. Roll in fine cracker crumbs and fry a golden brown in deep hot Cottolene. Drain on brown paper.

RHUBARB TARTS

If rhubarb is pink, young and tender, simply wash and cut in one-half inch pieces; there should be two and one-half cups. Cover with boiling water and heat to boiling point; boil five minutes. Do not allow it to lose its shape. Drain off all the juice, sprinkle rhubarb with three-fourths cup sugar. Sift over two tablespoons flour and one-fourth teaspoon salt, dot over with one tablespoon butter and a grating of orange rind. Mix well and turn into a pie pan lined with Rich Paste. Arrange strips of pastry, lattice-work fashion, across the top of pie and bake thirty minutes in a moderate oven.

Fifty-Two Sunday Dinners

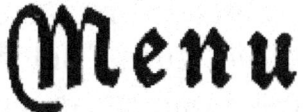

Strawberry Cocktails

Chicken Bouillon Chantilly

Fricassee of Chicken with Waffles

Spinach with Eggs

Prune and Pecan Nut Salad

Apricot Marmalade Mold

Cocoanut Cake

Coffee

CHICKEN BOUILLON CHANTILLY

Pour six cups of hot, well-seasoned Chicken Bouillon into hot bouillon cups. Drop on top of each portion one tablespoon whipped cream delicately seasoned with salt, pepper and a few grains cayenne. Sprinkle cream with paprika or finely chopped chives.

FRICASSEE OF CHICKEN

Dress, singe, clean and cut two young chickens in pieces for serving. Sprinkle with salt and pepper, and dredge with flour, brown richly in equal parts of Cottolene and butter, turning often that pieces may be evenly browned. Then cover with boiling water to which add a bit of bay leaf, one-half teaspoon peppercorns, a spray of parsley, six slices carrot and three slices onion. Cover and simmer until chicken is tender (from one to one and one-quarter hours). Remove chicken from stock, cover and keep warm; strain stock; there should be two cups. Melt four tablespoons butter in a sauce pan, add four tablespoons flour, stir to a paste, then gradually pour on the two cups hot stock, stirring constantly; let simmer ten minutes. Remove from range, add one cup of hot cream and the yolks of two eggs slightly beaten. Reheat chicken in sauce (do not allow sauce to boil after adding yolks). Serve with Waffles.

SPINACH WITH DEVILED EGGS

1 peck spinach.
¼ pound bacon.
Salt, pepper.
1/3 cup butter.
Few grains nutmeg.
5 hard-cooked eggs.
½ teaspoon salt.
¼ teaspoon pepper.
½ teaspoon finely chopped parsley.
½ teaspoon grated onion.
½ cup minced ham.
Cream Salad Dressing.

PROCESS: Cook spinach in the usual way. Cook the bacon with spinach to give it flavor. When spinach is tender, remove bacon, drain spinach and chop fine. Season with salt, pepper and nutmeg. Add butter, mix well and pack into an oval mold. Keep hot over hot water, cut eggs in halves lengthwise, remove yolks and rub through a sieve. Add ham, salt, pepper, parsley and onion juice. Moisten with Cream Salad Dressing to bind mixture together. Refill halves of eggs with this mixture, heaping it pyramid-like. Turn mold of spinach on hot serving dish and surround with stuffed eggs.

PRUNE AND NUT SALAD

Buy very select prunes for this purpose (tins holding one or two pounds are best), cook prunes in the usual way, letting the liquor evaporate during the latter part of cooking. Prunes should not be as well done as when serving them as sauce. Drain prunes from the liquor and chill them. Remove the stones carefully, cut prunes in five pieces lengthwise. Cut pecan nut meats in four pieces lengthwise. Mix prunes and nut meats, sprinkle with salt and paprika. For one-half pound prunes and one-fourth pound shelled nut meats allow one cup whipping cream. Whip cream until solid, season with one-half teaspoon each salt and paprika; add two tablespoons lemon juice and one and one-half tablespoons Sherry wine slowly, while beating constantly. Mix two-thirds of the cream with the prunes and nuts. Arrange the heart leaves of lettuce on cold, individual salad plates, pile some of the mixture in each and mask with remaining whipped cream. Arrange three pieces of prunes on top of each portion, radiating from center, and place a cherry or strawberry on top of each.

STEAMED SNOW BALLS

(For recipe, see page 168.)

COCOANUT CAKE

$2/3$ cup Cottolene.
2 cups sugar.
3 eggs.
3 cups flour.
5 teaspoons baking powder.
¼ teaspoon salt.
1 cup milk.
½ teaspoon each lemon and vanilla.

Process: Cream Cottolene, add one cup sugar gradually, stirring constantly. Beat yolks thick and light, add remaining cup sugar gradually, continue beating. Combine mixtures. Mix and sift flour, baking powder and salt. Add to first mixture alternately with milk. Add vanilla and fold in the whites of eggs beaten stiff and dry. Turn into two well-greased, square cake pans and bake fifteen minutes in a moderate oven. Spread one layer thickly with Boiled Frosting, sprinkle heavily with fresh grated cocoanut, cover with remaining layer. Spread top and sides with frosting, and sprinkle with cocoanut before frosting glazes.

BOILED FROSTING

2 cups sugar.
¼ teaspoon cream of tartar.
½ cup water.
Whites 2 eggs.

PROCESS: Mix sugar, cream of tartar and water in a sauce pan. Place on range and stir until mixture begins to boil. When syrup drops from the wooden spoon thick like honey, remove from range and add eight tablespoons of the syrup to the stiffly beaten whites of eggs, beating constantly. Return remaining syrup to range, continue cooking until syrup spins a thread at least five inches in length. Pour syrup in a thin stream onto first mixture and beat until cool and slightly glazed on side of bowl. Spread thickly on cake.

April
Second Sunday

Fifty-Two Sunday Dinners

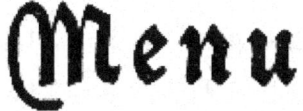

Smoked Sturgeon Canapé

Clam Broth   Buttered Wafers

Broiled Finnan Haddie

Potatoes on the Half Shell

Peggy's Sour Cabbage

Cheese Soufflé

Strawberry Shortcake

Coffee

SMOKED STURGEON CANAPÉ

Cut stale white bread in one-third inch slices, trim off crust and cut slices in crescents or triangles—then sauté a golden brown in butter. Spread with Anchovy paste or with French mustard, then arrange flaked smoked sturgeon over canapés. Sprinkle thickly with finely chopped olives and pimentos. Garnish each with a rolled fillet of Anchovy. Dispose each canapé on a bread and butter plate covered with a paper doily and garnish with sprays of parsley.

CLAM BOUILLON

1 peck of clams (in the shells).
3 cups cold water.

A Book of Recipes

Salt, pepper.
Whipped cream.

Process: Wash and scrub clams with a stiff brush, changing the water until no sand is seen in bottom of vessel. Put in a kettle, add cold water, cover closely and bring water gradually to boiling point, steam until all the shells are opened. Remove clam with shells, strain broth through double cheese-cloth, season and serve hot in hot bouillon cups. Drop a spoonful of whipped cream on top of each service and sprinkle with paprika.

BROILED FINNAN HADDIE

Wash the fish thoroughly; lay in a dripping pan, flesh side down; cover with cold water and let soak one hour. Drain; cover with hot water, let soak fifteen minutes. Drain again and wipe dry; brush over with soft butter and broil fifteen minutes over a slow fire or some distance from the flame if cooked with gas. Remove to hot serving platter and spread with Maître d'Hôtel Butter.

POTATOES ON THE HALF SHELL

Select smooth, large, uniform sized potatoes; wash and scrub them carefully with a brush. Bake and cut them in halves lengthwise; scoop out the pulp from shells, being careful not to break them. Press pulp through a ricer; season with salt, pepper, butter and hot cream. Add one teaspoon finely chopped parsley (to five potatoes), whip mixture until fluffy, refill shells with mixture, using pastry bag and rose tube. Place in oven until heated through. Dispose around Finnan Haddie, interspersed with sprays of parsley.

PEGGY'S SOUR CABBAGE

Select a small, firm head of white cabbage; cut in quarters, remove the tough stalk and shave crosswise as fine as possible. Put cabbage in a large frying pan, cover with water, cover closely and cook until cabbage is tender (from forty to eighty minutes). Season with salt the last fifteen minutes of cooking. Drain and add one-third to one-half cup of butter, toss cabbage until well buttered, sauté until some of the cabbage is delicately browned. Season with pepper, and add vinegar to taste. Serve hot.

CHEESE SOUFFLÉ

2 tablespoons butter.
3 tablespoons flour.
½ teaspoon salt.
$\frac{1}{8}$ teaspoon ground mustard.
¼ teaspoon paprika.
½ cup scalded milk.
¼ cup grated American cheese.
Yolks 3 eggs beaten thick and light.
Whites 3 eggs beaten stiff.

PROCESS: Melt butter in a saucepan; add flour mixed with seasonings, stir to a smooth paste and add gradually scalded milk, stirring constantly. Add grated cheese and when cheese is melted remove from range; add yolks of eggs and continue beating, then cut and fold in the whites of eggs. Turn mixture into a well-greased, one-quart baking dish and bake in a moderate oven twenty minutes. Serve at once.

STRAWBERRY SHORTCAKE

2 cups flour.
¾ teaspoon salt.
4 teaspoons baking powder.
2 tablespoons Cottolene.
1 cup thin cream.

Process: Sift together flour, salt and baking powder. Rub shortening in with tips of fingers. Add cream, mix with a knife to a soft dough. Turn on a floured board, knead slightly and divide the dough into two equal parts. Pat and roll each piece to one-half inch thickness; lay one piece in a buttered jelly cake pan, brush over with soft butter and place remaining piece on top. Bake in a hot oven fifteen minutes. Remove from oven; invert cake on a hot serving platter. Remove bottom layer (which is now the top). Spread with soft butter and add a layer of berries prepared as directed hereafter. Sift generously with bar sugar, replace remaining cake, cover with berries, sprinkle with sugar, mask with whipped cream sweetened and flavored with orange extract.

STRAWBERRY MIXTURE

Wash two quarts strawberries; hull and cut each berry in half. Prepare a syrup by boiling together two cups sugar and one-half cup water four minutes, cool and pour syrup over berries, or sprinkle raw sugar over berries and let stand one hour. Lift the berries from syrup and place between layer and on top of short cake. Strain syrup into a pitcher or bowl and pass with each portion of short cake.

April
Third Sunday

Fifty-Two Sunday Dinners

#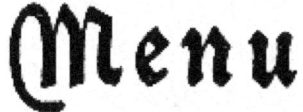

CREAM OF ASPARAGUS

BREADED MUTTON CHOPS—SAUCE SIGNORA

BAKED BANANAS—SULTANA SAUCE

FRIED WHOLE POTATOES   LETTUCE HEARTS

STEAMED GRAHAM PUDDING—SHERRY SAUCE

CAFÉ NOIR

BREADED MUTTON CHOPS

Wipe and trim chops, sprinkle with salt, pepper, and dredge with flour. Dip in egg diluted with cold water or milk (allowing two tablespoons to each egg), then in fine bread crumbs, repeat if not well coated with crumbs. Fry in deep hot Cottolene about ten minutes. Drain on brown paper and serve in a border of hot Mashed Potatoes with Green Pepper, or in a nest of Green Peas dressed with Maître d'Hôtel Butter.

SAUCE SIGNORA

Cook two tablespoons of chopped, lean, raw ham in one-fourth cup butter until lightly browned, add one-fourth cup flour, one-half teaspoon salt, and stir until well blended, then add one and one-half cups of Brown Stock and one cup of Chili Sauce. Heat to boiling point, stirring constantly. Reduce heat and simmer ten minutes. This sauce may be strained or served without straining. Care must be taken that ham is not overcooked.

A Book of Recipes

BAKED BANANAS WITH SULTANA SAUCE

    6 bananas.
    ¾ cup Sultana raisins.
    2-¾ cups boiling water.
    1 cup sugar.
    1 tablespoon butter.
    Few grains salt.
    ¼ cup Sherry wine.
    2 tablespoons lemon juice.
    1 tablespoon cornstarch or two teaspoons Arrowroot.

PROCESS: With a sharp knife open and peel down one section of each banana, carefully loosen the pulp from the rest of the skin; remove pulp and scrape lightly with a silver knife, removing all the coarse threads. Replace the pulp in its original shape in the skins. Arrange the bananas in an agate dripping pan and bake in a moderate oven until the skins are black and the pulp is soft (from ten to fifteen minutes). Remove pulp from skins to serving platter, being careful to preserve their shape. Curve them slightly and pour over

SULTANA SAUCE

Pick over raisins, cover them with water and cook until raisins are tender. Mix sugar, cornstarch and salt, add slowly to raisins and water, stirring constantly. Cook slowly twenty minutes; add butter, lemon juice and wine. Reheat and serve.

FRIED WHOLE POTATOES

Select small potatoes of uniform size. Wash, pare and parboil in boiling salted water ten minutes. Drain dry and fry a golden brown in deep hot Cottolene (time required about twelve minutes). Fat should not be hot enough to brown potatoes until the last five minutes of cooking, otherwise potatoes will not be cooked throughout. Drain on brown paper, sprinkle with salt and serve at once.

STEAMED GRAHAM PUDDING

3 tablespoons Cottolene.
½ cup N. O. Molasses.
½ cup milk.
1 egg well beaten.
1½ cups Graham flour.
½ teaspoon soda.
1 teaspoon salt.
½ teaspoon cinnamon.
¼ teaspoon cloves.
½ teaspoon mace.
1 cup dates stoned and cut in pieces.

PROCESS: Cream Cottolene, add molasses, milk and egg. Mix and sift the dry ingredients, add dates and stir into first mixture, beat thoroughly. Turn into a buttered tube mold, cover and steam two and one-half hours. Serve with Sherry Sauce (recipe Page 130).

April
Fourth Sunday

Fifty-Two Sunday Dinners

##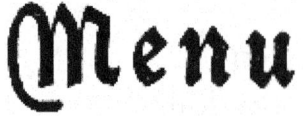

Spanish Soup

Baked Halibut

Potatoes à l'Aurora

Corn Fritters   Cabbage Relish

Stewed Rhubarb with Pineapple and Raisins

Old Fashioned Marble Cake

SPANISH SOUP

4 cups Brown Stock.
2 cups tomato pulp.
1 large, green, finely chopped pepper.
1 medium-sized onion, finely chopped.
4 tablespoons butter.
5 tablespoons flour.
2 tablespoons freshly grated horseradish.
½ tablespoon Worcestershire Sauce.
Salt, pepper and cayenne, or
A few drops Tobasco Sauce.
½ cup hot cooked rice.

Process: Cook pepper and onion in butter five minutes. Add flour, stir until well blended and delicately browned, then add gradually stock and tomato pulp; let simmer twenty minutes. Rub through a sieve and season

A Book of Recipes

highly with salt, pepper, and cayenne or Tobasco. Before serving add Worcestershire, horseradish and rice.

BAKED HALIBUT

Wipe a two-pound slice of halibut. Arrange six or eight thin slices of fat salt pork in bottom of dripping pan, slice an onion thinly over pork, add a bit of bay leaf and arrange halibut over onion. Spread halibut evenly with a butter paste made of four tablespoons butter worked to a cream with three tablespoons flour. Season with one-half teaspoon salt and a few grains cayenne. Over butter paste sprinkle thickly-buttered cracker crumbs, and arrange alternately strips of pimento and thin slices of bacon over crumbs. Cover with a buttered paper and bake slowly one hour in a moderate oven. Remove paper the last fifteen minutes of cooking to brown the crumbs and bacon delicately. Remove to hot serving platter and garnish with shredded potatoes, sliced lemon and parsley.

POTATOES AURORA

Cut cold, boiled potatoes in one-fourth inch cubes. There should be sufficient to fill three cups. Reheat potatoes in two cups of thin white sauce, turn into hot serving dish. Remove the shells from four hard-cooked eggs, cut them in halves crosswise, remove the yolks. Cut whites in rings and arrange rings around edge of potatoes; press the yolks through a ricer over potatoes. Sprinkle the rings with finely chopped parsley. Serve at once.

CORN FRITTERS

1 can corn, chopped fine.
1 cup flour.
1 teaspoon baking powder.
1 teaspoon sugar.
2 teaspoons salt.
¼ teaspoon white pepper.
2 eggs.

PROCESS: Add dry ingredients, sifted together, to corn; add yolks well beaten; then fold in whites beaten until stiff. Fry as griddle cakes; or dip a tablespoon into deep hot Cottolene, drain well, then take up a spoonful of the corn mixture, drop into hot Cottolene, pushing it off spoon into hot fat with a spatula. Fry a golden brown. Drain on brown paper and serve immediately.

CABBAGE RELISH

Remove the wilted and coarse outside leaves from one small, solid head of white, new cabbage (Southern), cut off stalk, cut head in quarters, cut out stalk from each quarter and chop cabbage very fine. Add one medium-sized Bermuda onion, finely chopped. Cover with ice water and let stand until crisp. Drain thoroughly and mix with Relish Dressing. Serve in lemon baskets, sprinkle with finely chopped chives, green pepper or parsley.

RELISH DRESSING

1 teaspoon mustard.
1½ teaspoons salt.
½ tablespoon flour.
1 tablespoon sugar.
Few grains cayenne.
1 tablespoon melted butter.
1 egg yolk.
$1/3$ cup hot vinegar.
½ teaspoon celery seed.
$2/3$ cup thick cream.

PROCESS: Mix the ingredients, except celery seed, in the order given. Cook in double boiler, stirring constantly until mixture coats the spoon; strain and add celery seed. Chill and add to cabbage.

STEWED RHUBARB

Wash and trim off ends of two pounds tender rhubarb; do not peel. Cut rhubarb in one-inch pieces. Put into baking dish and sprinkle generously with sugar, add just enough water to prevent rhubarb from burning. Cover and bake in oven very slowly until tender but not broken. (Slow cooking preserves its color.) One cup of Sultana raisins may be cooked with rhubarb. They must, however, be first picked over, stems removed, then covered with boiling water, drained, then covered again with boiling water and cooked until soft. Arrange a layer of rhubarb in baking dish, then a sprinkle of raisins and sugar and thus continue until all are used. Finish cooking as directed in the foregoing. Serve very cold.

MARBLE CAKE

$1/3$ cup Cottolene.
1 cup sugar.
2 eggs.
½ cup milk.
½ teaspoon cinnamon.
½ teaspoon nutmeg.
¼ teaspoon salt.
1-¾ cups flour.
3 teaspoons baking powder.
1 tablespoon molasses.

PROCESS: Cream Cottolene, add sugar gradually, yolks of eggs beaten until thick and light, flour sifted with baking powder, alternately with milk. Fold in whites of eggs beaten until stiff. Turn one-third of this batter into a bowl and add to it molasses and spices. Pour into well-greased pan, alternating light and dark mixtures to give it the "marbled" appearance.

Bake forty to forty-five minutes in a moderate oven.

"If you are an artist in the kitchen you will always be esteemed."—

#

Asparagus Soup—Saltines

Baked Bluefish à la Creole

Chateau Potatoes   Stringless Beans with Bacon

Cheese and Pimento Salad

Frozen Strawberries

Corn-Starch Loaf Cake with Maple Frosting

Café Noir—Tea Frappé

CREAM OF ASPARAGUS SOUP
3 cups White Stock.
1 bunch (or 1 can) asparagus.
2 cups cold water.
2 slices onion.
4 tablespoons butter.
4 tablespoons flour.
1½ cups scalded milk.
½ cup hot cream.

Process: Wash, scrape and cut asparagus in one-inch pieces, reserve the tips. Cover with boiling salted water, cook ten minutes; drain, add stock and onion and cook until tender, rub through a sieve. Melt butter in a sauce pan, add flour, stir to a smooth paste; remove from fire and add first mixture slowly, stirring constantly. Season with salt and pepper, add hot milk and cream, continue stirring. Cook tips in boiling salted water until tender, drain. Turn soup into hot soup tureen, add tips and serve. If canned asparagus is used, drain from liquor, rinse, reserve tips and follow directions given in the foregoing.

BLUEFISH À LA CREOLE

Remove bones from a fresh, three-pound bluefish. Place on a well-buttered fish sheet, laid in a dripping pan. Sprinkle with salt and paprika. Cook in a hot oven twenty-five minutes, basting often with melted butter or sweet dripping. Remove to hot serving platter and pour a Creole Sauce around fish. Sprinkle fish with buttered crumbs, set platter on a board and place in oven to brown crumbs. Garnish with slices of lemon dipped in chopped parsley.

CREOLE SAUCE

(For recipe see Page 122.)

CHATEAU POTATOES

Wash, pare and cook (almost soft) one-half dozen medium-size potatoes. Drain perfectly dry, cool and cut them in quarters, trim them in the shape of small gherkins. Wash them in cold water, then put them in a frying pan, reheat in boiling water. Drain and add four tablespoons butter; shake the pan until potatoes are well buttered and a golden brown color. Remove carefully with a skimmer to hot serving dish, and sprinkle with finely chopped parsley.

STRINGLESS BEANS WITH BACON

Cut three thin slices of bacon in shreds crosswise, try out in a frying pan. Cook until tender two cups green, stringless beans and three or four small new onions, in boiling salted water. Drain and add to bacon, mix well, add salt (if necessary) and pepper; turn into a hot serving dish.

CHEESE AND PIMENTO SALAD

(For recipe see Page 26.)

FROZEN STRAWBERRIES

4 cups thin cream.
3 cups thick cream.
2 cups milk.
1 cup sugar.
¼ cup water.
Few grains salt.
2 cups strawberry juice and pulp.
1 tablespoon lemon juice.
Strawberries.

Process: Cook water and sugar together three minutes. Cool and add to cream and milk. Add a sprinkle of salt. Turn into freezer and when half frozen add lemon juice and strawberry pulp. Finish freezing. Let stand an hour or two to ripen. Serve in cone shape and place a large, unhulled strawberry in top of each cone.

CORN STARCH LOAF CAKE

⅔ cup Cottolene.
2 cups fine sugar.
1 cup milk.
1 cup corn starch.
2 cups flour.
1½ tablespoons baking powder.
Whites 5 eggs beaten stiff.
½ teaspoon salt.
1 teaspoon vanilla.

Process: Cream Cottolene, add sugar gradually, stirring constantly. Mix and sift flour, corn starch, baking powder and salt; add alternately to first mixture with milk, add vanilla, then cut and fold in whites of eggs. Turn mixture into two well-greased, brick-shaped bread pans and bake forty-five minutes in a moderate oven. Spread with Maple Frosting (see Page 103) and stick with blanched and shredded almonds slightly toasted.

Menu

CREAM OF SPINACH   CROUTONS

YOUNG PIGEONS (STALL FED) STUFFED AND BRAISED

MASHED POTATOES   ASPARAGUS WITH BUTTER SAUCE

SPINACH SALAD

COTTAGE PUDDING WITH STRAWBERRIES

COFFEE

CREAM OF SPINACH

½ peck spinach.
6 cups cold water.
½ small bay leaf.
1½ teaspoons salt.
3 tablespoons Cottolene.
2 cups milk.
2 slices onion.
3 tablespoons flour.
½ cup heavy cream.
Cayenne pepper and celery salt.

PROCESS: Cook spinach in water thirty minutes. Drain, chop, and rub through sieve. Scald milk with onion and bay leaf. Melt Cottolene in saucepan, add flour, stir to a smooth paste, pour on slowly scalded milk (first removing onion and bay leaf), stirring constantly. Add seasonings, spinach pulp; cook five minutes and serve with cream, whipped stiff. Sprinkle each portion with finely chopped parsley.

YOUNG PIGEONS STUFFED AND BRAISED

Clean, stuff and truss six *young* pigeons. Arrange them in a stew pan or Dutch oven. Add one quart boiling water; add three blades celery, cut in pieces, and three slices of onion, a small bit of bay leaf and one-half teaspoon peppercorns. Cover closely and simmer (in the oven if Dutch oven is used) slowly, until birds are tender (about two hours according to age of birds). Remove from casserole, cool and spread with soft butter. Sprinkle with salt, pepper, and dredge with flour. Strain liquor from casserole. Try out fat salt pork in vessel, and brown birds richly in the pork fat, turning often that they may be evenly browned. Make a sauce of the strained stock. Make shallow, boat-shape croutons of stale bread, fry them a golden brown in deep hot Cottolene, drain on brown paper and arrange a bird in each boat. Garnish with parsley.

STUFFING FOR PIGEONS

1 cup hot, riced potato.
½ teaspoon salt.
$\frac{1}{8}$ teaspoon pepper.
1 teaspoon finely chopped chives.
1 tablespoon butter.
¼ cup soft stale bread crumbs soaked in water then wrung in a napkin.
1 egg yolk.
Few grains poultry seasonings.

PROCESS: Mix ingredients in the order given and fill body of pigeons.

ASPARAGUS WITH BUTTER SAUCE

Untie the bunches, wash and remove scales. Cut off the hard part of spears as far up as they will snap. Retie, and cook in boiling salted water until tender (about fifteen minutes), leaving the tips out of water the first ten minutes of cooking. Drain, remove strings. Arrange in hot serving dish and pour over two tablespoons melted butter (for each bunch), sprinkle with salt and pepper.

SPINACH SALAD

Pick over and wash in several waters or until no sand is left in bottom of bowl, one-half peck spinach. Drain and cook in its own juice and the water that clings to the leaves (if spinach is old, cook it in plenty of water), until soft. Drain dry as possible and chop finely. Season with salt, pepper and Tarragon vinegar. Cut bacon in shreds crosswise, then cut shreds in small bits. Sauté them until delicately browned and crisp, skim them from the fat, add them to spinach, add one tablespoon of bacon fat. Butter lightly small Dairole molds and pack solidly with spinach. Chill, unmold and arrange on thin slices of cold, boiled ham, tongue or Bologna sausage, trimmed in circular pieces a trifle larger than mold of spinach. Arrange each portion in a nest of parsley or cress, and fill depression on top of spinach with Mayonnaise or Sauce Tartare (for recipe see Page 84).

May
Third Sunday

Fifty-Two Sunday Dinners

#

CREAM OF ASPARAGUS

BRAISED CALF'S LIVER

RICE AU GRATIN   CARROTS AND TURNIPS IN CREAM SAUCE

ASPARAGUS SALAD

CUSTARD PIE   EDAM CHEESE

COFFEE

ICED TEA

CREAM OF ASPARAGUS

(For recipe see Page 66.)

BRAISED CALF'S LIVER

Wipe liver and skewer into shape, if necessary. Draw small lardoons through the liver, in parallel rows, leaving each lardoon extend one-half inch above surface. Place liver in a casserole or Dutch oven, surround with remnants of lardoons. Sprinkle with salt, pepper and dredge with flour. Surround with one-third cup each of carrots, onion and celery, cut in small cubes; add one-half teaspoon peppercorns, six cloves, one spray parsley, a bit of bay leaf and two cups hot Brown Stock or water. Cover closely and cook in a slow oven two hours. Remove cover the last half hour of cooking that liver may brown richly. Remove liver to serving platter, set aside in a warm place. Strain liquor in casserole and use for making a Brown Sauce. Pour sauce around liver and serve. Braised liver may be served cold, thinly sliced.

RICE AU GRATIN

1½ cups steamed or boiled rice.
1 tablespoon salt.
1½ tablespoons butter.
$\frac{1}{3}$ lb. grated cheese.
Cayenne.
Milk.
Buttered cracker crumbs.

Process: When steaming or boiling the rice, allow one tablespoon of salt for seasoning. Butter a baking dish and cover with a layer of rice, dot over with some of the butter. Sprinkle with a thin layer of cheese and a slight sprinkle cayenne; repeat alternate layers until rice and cheese are used. Pour on milk to half the depth of baking dish, cover with buttered cracker crumbs and bake in oven until cheese melts and crumbs are brown.

CARROTS AND TURNIPS IN CREAM SAUCE

Scrub, scrape and cut carrots in small cubes. Wash, pare and cut purple-top turnips the same. (There should be one and one-half cups of each.) Cover each (in separate vessels) with boiling water and cook until tender; add salt the last half hour of cooking. Drain well, toss together and reheat in one and one-half cups Thin White Sauce.

ASPARAGUS SALAD

Cook asparagus in the usual way, drain and slip three or four spears through an onion ring just large enough to hold them. Arrange these fagots in nests of crisp lettuce heart leaves. Just before serving pour over French Dressing to which has been added one tablespoon of finely chopped chives. A band of red or green pepper may be used in place of the onion ring. Canned asparagus should first be drained from the liquor in the can then rinsed with cold water. Chilled and served as directed in the foregoing.

CUSTARD PIE

Line a deep, perforated pie tin with Plain or Rich Paste. For filling, beat three eggs slightly, add one-fourth cup sugar, one-eighth teaspoon salt, one-eighth teaspoon nutmeg, and pour over slowly two cups scalded milk, stirring constantly. Bake in a hot oven at first, to set the crust or rim, then reduce the heat afterwards; as this is a combination of eggs and milk it should be finished in a slow oven.

May
Fourth Sunday

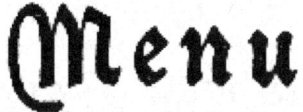

CONSOMMÉ—BREAD STICKS

BOILED CORNED BEEF WITH VEGETABLES

DANDELION SALAD

FROZEN STRAWBERRIES

SPANISH LAYER CAKE

CAFÉ NOIR—ICED TEA

CONSOMMÉ WITH BREAD STICKS

(For recipe see Page 149.)

BOILED CORNED BEEF WITH VEGETABLES

Select five or six pounds from the plate or the brisket; wash carefully in cold water, drain; place in kettle and cover with boiling water, let boil five minutes and—if very briny—drain, rinse off scum with hot water and again cover with boiling water; heat to boiling point and simmer until meat is tender (about six hours). Remove beef from liquor, keep covered in a warm place. Skim off some of the fat from liquor. Add carrots washed, scraped and cut in quarters. Let cook fifteen minutes, then add small white onions and turnips pared and cut in quarters, one head white cabbage cut in quarters (stalk cut out). Wash, pare and cut uniform-sized potatoes in quarters, parboil five minutes, then drain and add to other ingredients. Cook beets in a separate vessel. When vegetables are soft, arrange meat in center of hot serving platter and surround with carrots, turnips, onions and cabbage. Sprinkle vegetables with finely chopped parsley, serve beets in separate dish. Pass horseradish, mustard and vinegar.

DANDELION SALAD

Gather the dandelion when young and tender. That which is cultivated is well bleached and very tender. Wash thoroughly in several waters, cut off the roots and outside leaves. Drain dry on a cloth or in a wire basket. Arrange in salad bowl. Cut thin sweet bacon in tiny shreds crosswise and sauté in frying pan until crisp; sprinkle bacon over dandelion. To the fat in pan (there should be one-third cup), add one-fourth cup vinegar diluted with two tablespoons water. Heat to boiling point and pour over dandelions; toss leaves with a fork until well mixed with dressing; serve at once.

FROZEN STRAWBERRIES—No. 2

2 quarts cream.
2 cups sugar.
Few grains salt.
2 cups strawberry juice and pulp.

PROCESS: Wash and hull strawberries (about three boxes); sprinkle with one cup sugar, cover closely and set aside in a cool place for two hours. Mash and squeeze berries through cheese cloth. Mix remaining cup sugar and salt with cream; turn into freezer and, when half frozen, add strawberries and finish freezing. Serve with Strawberry Sauce.

STRAWBERRY SAUCE

1 cup sugar.
$1/3$ cup water.
2 cups strawberry pulp.

PROCESS: Make a syrup by boiling water with sugar three minutes (after mixture begins to boil), cool slightly and add strawberry pulp. Chill thoroughly and serve.

SPANISH LAYER CAKE

$1/3$ cup Cottolene.
1 cup sugar.

Yolks 2 eggs.
½ cup milk.
1⅞ cups pastry flour.
3 teaspoons baking powder.
1 teaspoon cinnamon.
¼ teaspoon cloves.
¼ teaspoon salt.
Whites 2 eggs.

PROCESS: Cream Cottolene, add sugar gradually, stirring constantly. Mix and sift flour, baking powder, spices and salt; add to first mixture alternately with milk. Cut and fold in stiffly beaten whites of eggs. Bake in two well-greased, square, layer cake pans. Spread with a thick layer of raspberry between layers. Cover top with frosting or dredge with powdered sugar.

May
Fifth Sunday

Fifty-Two Sunday Dinners

#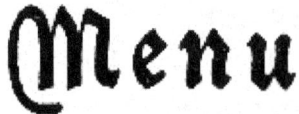

Cream of Rice Soup

Flank Steak Stuffed and Braised

Boiled Rice   Dandelion Greens with Bacon

Asparagus Salad

Strawberry Short Cake

Café Noir

CREAM OF RICE SOUP

1 cup rice, well washed.
1½ quarts cold water.
1 onion sliced.
1 green pepper cut in shreds.
2 cups hot cream or milk.
¼ cup butter.
2 tablespoons flour.
Salt, cayenne and nutmeg.
1 teaspoon finely chopped parsley.

Process: Heat water to boiling, season with salt and add rice, onion and green pepper (discarding seeds and veins). Cook until rice is soft; rub through a sieve. Melt butter in a saucepan, add flour, stir to a smooth paste, add cream slowly, stirring constantly. Add seasonings and cook over hot water ten minutes. Combine with rice mixture, continue cooking five minutes. Turn into hot soup tureen and sprinkle over with parsley.

A Book of Recipes

FLANK STEAK STUFFED AND BRAISED

Select a flank steak weighing about two and one-half pounds. Have the butcher peel off the superfluous fat and tissue and score both sides diagonally in opposite directions. Remove the steak from paper when it comes from market and lay it flat on meat board, sprinkle with salt and pepper. Spread over it a thin layer of stuffing, (see Page 154), roll lengthwise, very compactly, sew the overlapping edge securely, also the ends. Sprinkle roll with salt, pepper and dredge with flour. Place meat in pan with enough Cottolene to brown it richly, turning roll until it is richly browned all over. Then remove to Dutch oven or casserole; rinse dripping pan with a little boiling water, pour over meat and surround with two cups stewed and strained tomato pulp, one onion thinly sliced, one green pepper shredded (after removing seeds and veins), two sprays parsley, the half of a small bay leaf and two tablespoons Worcestershire sauce. Cover closely, place in oven and cook meat very slowly about three to four hours. Remove meat to serving platter. Dilute four tablespoons flour with cold water to the consistency to pour, add to sauce in pan, stir until well blended, season with salt and pepper; let simmer ten minutes, then strain around meat. Garnish with sprays of parsley or cress.

DANDELION GREENS

Remove the roots, carefully pick over (discarding all tough and wilted leaves) and wash dandelion leaves in several waters; to the last water add salt to free leaves from insects and vermin. It will require one peck of leaves to serve a family of six. Cook leaves in plenty of boiling salted water until tender; drain at once and chop fine. Dress with butter and pepper; cut thin slices of bacon in shreds crosswise, try it out and pour over dandelions. (There should be one-third cup bacon fat.) The shreds of bacon are an attractive garnish; hard-cooked eggs may also be used as a garnish. Cut them in eighths or rings. Vinegar is sometimes added. Serve hot.

STRAWBERRY SHORT CAKE

(For recipe see Page 59.)

Fifty-Two Sunday Dinners

#

CONSOMMÉ   BROWNED CRACKERS

LAMB CHOPS BREADED—MAÎTRE D'HÔTEL BUTTER

NEW POTATOES   CHIVE SAUCE

GREEN PEAS

JUNE SALAD

CHERRY PIE

ICED TEA—CAFÉ NOIR

CONSOMMÉ PRINCESS

Add to Consommé small green peas and tiny cubes of cold cooked breast of chicken. (For recipe for Consommé see Page 149.)

BROWNED CRACKERS

Split crackers, arrange them in a dripping pan, place in a moderate oven until crisp and delicately browned.

LAMB CHOPS BREADED

Prepare loin or French chops as for broiling. Dip in crumbs, egg (diluted with cold water, allowing two tablespoons water to each egg), add in crumbs, and fry in deep hot Cottolene six to eight minutes. Drain on brown paper and spread with Maître d'Hôtel Butter.

A Book of Recipes

NEW POTATOES WITH CHIVE SAUCE

Scrape off the skin, remove the "eyes" with a sharp pointed knife and scrub them with a vegetable brush, rinse thoroughly and put in sauce pan, add boiling water to cover; season with salt, cover and cook until soft, drain. If small, serve whole; if large, cut them in one-half inch cubes and reheat in Chive Sauce.

CHIVE SAUCE

To Cream Sauce (see Page 151) add one tablespoon finely chopped Chives.

GREEN PEAS

Cook peas in boiling water. Use just enough water to prevent them from burning. Add salt fifteen minutes before removing them from fire. Season with butter and pepper.

JUNE SALAD

Remove stones from red and pink Ox-heart cherries and cut them in halves lengthwise. Remove the pulp from oranges and cut in inch cubes; peel bananas and cut in one-half inch cubes. Use equal quantities of each and marinate with French Dressing No. 2. Serve in nests of heart lettuce leaves and mask with Mayonnaise.

FRENCH DRESSING No. 2

¼ teaspoon salt.
4 tablespoons Olive oil.
$\frac{1}{8}$ teaspoon paprika.
2 tablespoons lemon juice.

PROCESS: Put seasoning in small bowl, add oil slowly, stirring constantly; add lemon juice slowly, continue beating until all is used. Chill, beat again and turn over fruit.

MAYONNAISE DRESSING

½ teaspoon salt.
Few grains cayenne.

Yolks 2 eggs.
1½ tablespoons lemon juice, or
¾ tablespoon each of vinegar and lemon juice.
¾ cup Olive oil.

PROCESS: Put seasoning in bowl, add egg yolks and mix thoroughly, add oil drop by drop, until four tablespoons have been added, after which larger quantities may be added. Stir constantly. As mixture thickens, add a teaspoon lemon juice or vinegar. Continue adding oil and lemon juice or vinegar alternately until all is used, stirring constantly. All ingredients should be very cold. Set bowl in which dressing is made in a bowl of crushed ice.

CHERRY PIE

Pick over, stem and pit cherries (there should be two cups when pitted). Heat to boiling point in their own juice, then chill them. Line a perforated pie pan with Rich Paste, moisten the rim with cold water and lay around a strip of pastry one inch wide, press lightly. Brush the pastry over with slightly beaten white of egg. Sweeten cherries to taste, add a few grains of salt and turn into lined pie pan. Sift over two tablespoons flour, moisten rim and cover with top crust, flute the edges and bake in hot oven for the first ten minutes, then reduce heat, continue baking for twenty-five minutes. Serve hot with cheese, cut in strips one-fourth inch thick and wide by two and one-half inches long.

ICED TEA

Make tea and chill. Serve in glasses filled with crushed ice, adding (if desired) one tablespoon lemon juice to each glass. Pass fine granulated (Bar) sugar. Place each glass on a small plate.

Menu

CHEESE CANAPÉS

HAMBURG ROAST—BROWN SAUCE

ROAST NEW POTATOES

GREEN PEAS WITH NEW CARROTS IN CREAM SAUCE

GARDEN CRESS WITH ORANGES—FRENCH DRESSING

CURRANT PIE

COFFEE   CHERRY PUNCH

CHEESE CANAPÉS

Cut stale bread in one-quarter inch slices, shape with small biscuit cutter (2 inches in diameter). Spread lightly with French or German mustard, sprinkle thickly with grated cheese, sprinkle cheese with finely chopped olives. Place a small stuffed olive in center of each. Dispose on a small plate covered with a paper doily. Garnish with sprays of parsley and serve as an "appetizer."

HAMBURG ROAST

Remove the fat and stringy parts, also marrow-bone, from two pounds round steak. Pass through the meat grinder twice; add the marrow taken from bone, one tablespoon green pepper finely chopped, one tablespoon onion finely chopped, season well with salt and the beaten yolks of two eggs or one whole egg slightly beaten; add one-half cup of soft bread crumbs that have been soaked in cold water thirty minutes and wrung dry in a double cheese cloth. Mix ingredients thoroughly with the hand. Shape in a compact roll of uniform thickness. Lay thin slices of salt pork or bacon in the bottom of a dripping pan, set the roast on them; lay thin slices of salt pork over the meat and place in a hot oven. After the first eight minutes reduce the heat and baste with the hot fat in the pan; let cook about thirty minutes, basting every ten minutes. The roast should be richly browned on the outside and a delicate pink inside. Serve surrounded with Tomato, Brown or Creole Sauce.

BROWN SAUCE

2 tablespoons butter.
1 slice onion.
4 tablespoons flour.
1½ cups Brown Stock.
¼ teaspoon salt.
$1/8$ teaspoon pepper.

PROCESS: Melt butter in sauce pan, add onion and cook until delicately browned; remove onion, and cook butter until richly browned, stirring constantly; add flour sifted with seasonings, stir to a paste and continue browning. Then pour on stock, slowly stirring until smooth and glossy. Onion may be omitted.

ROAST NEW POTATOES

Select uniform-sized new potatoes, wash and scrub them with a brush, pare and parboil ten to fifteen minutes (according to the size) in boiling salted water. Drain and place them around rack in dripping pan in which meat is roasting and cook until tender. Baste occasionally with fat in pan when basting roast.

GREEN PEAS AND NEW CARROTS IN CREAM SAUCE

Cook one and one-half cups of peas in just enough water to prevent them from burning. Add salt fifteen minutes before removing them from range.

Wash, scrub and scrape new carrots and cut them in one-fourth inch cubes (there should be one and one-half cups); cook in boiling salted water until tender. Drain and mix with peas. Reheat them in one and one-half cups of Cream Sauce (for recipe see Page 151).

GARDEN CRESS WITH ORANGES

Arrange individual nests of Garden Cress on six chilled salad plates. Cut eight oranges in halves, remove the pulp, discarding veins and sections. Leave the pulp in the original shape as taken from the sections; divide the pulp evenly between the six nests. Serve with French Dressing and sprinkle each portion with paprika and a few grains cayenne. Omit the garlic when using fruit.

FRENCH DRESSING

½ teaspoon salt.
⅛ teaspoon pepper.
¼ teaspoon paprika.
6 tablespoons olive oil.
2 tablespoons vinegar.
Garlic.

Process: Rub the mixing bowl with a bruised clove of garlic; add salt, pepper, paprika and oil; beat until ingredients are thoroughly blended, adding vinegar slowly meanwhile. A piece of ice put into bowl while stirring will aid in chilling the mixture.

CURRANT PIE

2½ cups cleaned currants.
2 cups sugar.
⅛ teaspoon salt.
2 eggs slightly beaten.
2 tablespoons flour.

Process: Mix the ingredients in the order given. Turn in a lined pie pan, heaping currants in center; cover with top crust, press and flute the edges. Bake as other berry pies. Serve hot. Sprinkle with powdered sugar.

CHERRY PUNCH

Boil two cups sugar and one cup water until a rich syrup is formed. Add one cup of lemon juice and two cups of Cherry juice, left over when canning cherries. (This left-over juice may be brought to the boiling point, skimmed and turned into sterilized fruit jars, sealed and stored as canned fruit and may be used for punch or pudding sauce.) Add two cups cold water. Fill a claret pitcher with cracked ice; add mixture. When serving, place a thin slice of orange, three or four strawberries and three pitted California cherries in each glass, fill three-fourths full with mixture. Serve very cold.

#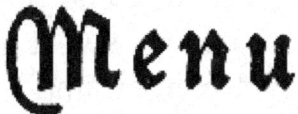

CHICKEN CONSOMMÉ WITH POACHED EGG YOLKS

FRIED PERCH—SAUCE TARTARE

SHREDDED POTATOES   ASPARAGUS ON TOAST

LETTUCE WITH CREAM DRESSING

CHERRY ROLY-POLY   CHERRY SAUCE

COFFEE

CHICKEN CONSOMMÉ WITH POACHED EGG YOLKS

Heat six cups of Chicken Consommé to the boiling point. Poach the yolks of six eggs in hot water until firm; remove from water with a skimmer. Place one yolk in each Bouillon cup and pour on hot consommé. Sprinkle slightly with finely chopped chives or parsley.

FRIED PERCH

Select fresh perch of medium size. Clean, bone and wipe dry as possible. Sprinkle with salt, pepper, dip in flour, egg, and crumbs (be sure fish are well coated with crumbs). Lay three at a time in a croquette basket and fry a golden brown in deep hot Cottolene. Cottolene should not be so hot as to brown fish at once, as fish will not be cooked through. (Time required for frying small fish is from four to six minutes.) Drain on brown paper and serve with Sauce Tartare. Garnish with parsley, lemon slices and radishes cut to imitate roses.

SAUCE TARTARE

To one cup of Mayonnaise Dressing add one finely chopped shallot, one tablespoon each finely chopped capers, sweet gherkins, olives, and one-half tablespoon each finely chopped parsley and fresh tarragon. Mix well and keep cool until ready to serve.

SHREDDED POTATOES

Wash, pare and cut potatoes in one-eighth inch slices. Cut slices in tiny straws. Wash carefully in cold water until water ceases to be cloudy. Let stand one hour in cold water. Drain and dry on towels. Fry a golden brown in deep hot Cottolene. Drain on brown paper, sprinkle with salt and serve around fried perch.

ASPARAGUS TIPS IN CROUSTADES

Prepare the asparagus in the usual way, cut off the tops one inch in length. Cook in as little boiling salted water as possible. Drain and dress with a Béchamel Sauce. Serve in Bread Croustades (small round, square, or diamond-shaped molds cut through thick slices of bread).

BÉCHAMEL SAUCE

4 tablespoons butter.
4 tablespoons flour.
1½ cups highly seasoned chicken stock.
½ cup hot thin cream.
Yolk 2 eggs.
Salt, pepper, few grains nutmeg.

Process: Melt butter in a saucepan, add flour, stir to a smooth paste; add stock slowly, stirring constantly; add cream and continue stirring. Bring to boiling point, remove from range and add egg yolk slightly beaten. Add seasonings. Beat until smooth and glossy. Keep hot over hot water. Do not allow sauce to boil after adding yolk of egg.

LETTUCE WITH CREAM DRESSING

Pick over, wash thoroughly young tender lettuce; cut off the roots and drain. Beat one-half cup heavy cream until solid. Add two tablespoons vinegar diluted with one tablespoon cold water. Add one tablespoon finely chopped chives, one-half teaspoon salt and one-eighth teaspoon pepper. Pour over lettuce, mix well and serve cold.

CHERRY ROLY-POLY

Make a baking powder biscuit dough as for Cream Fruit Rolls. (See Page 180.) Roll to one-half inch thickness. Drain pitted cherries from the juice; strew them over dough, sprinkle with sugar and dredge lightly with flour. Roll like a jelly roll, moisten and press the overlapping edge and close the ends as securely as possible. Bake in a hot oven, twenty-five minutes, basting three times with some of the cherry juice sweetened to taste, or tie loosely in a floured cloth and cook in boiling water two hours, or steam in a steamer one hour. Serve on a hot platter with Cherry Sauce.

CHERRY SAUCE

2 cups pitted cherries.
1 cup claret.
⅔ cup sugar.
½ glass red currant jelly.
Juice 1 lemon.
½ dozen Cassia buds.

PROCESS: Mix the ingredients in the order given, cook slowly until reduced to a syrup. Strain through a sieve and serve hot with Cherry Roly-Poly or Dumplings.

June
Fourth Sunday

Fifty-Two Sunday Dinners

Menu

Cream of Asparagus Soup—Croutons

Radishes   Green Onions

Roast Stuffed Shoulder of Lamb—Mint Sauce

New Potatoes with Peas

Swiss Chard with Bacon and "Hard Boiled" Eggs

Cherry Duff   Cherry Sauce

Coffee

CREAM OF ASPARAGUS SOUP

(For recipe see Page 66.)

CROUTONS

Cut stale bread in one-third inch slices; remove crusts and cut in one-third inch strips, cut strips in one-third inch cubes. Fry them a golden brown in deep hot Cottolene. Drain on brown paper and sprinkle lightly with salt.

ROAST SHOULDER OF LAMB

Order a shoulder and fore-leg of lamb, boned. Wipe, stuff and truss in shape. Sprinkle with salt, pepper and dredge with flour. Place on rack in dripping pan, put in hot oven and baste with dripping melted in one cup hot water, as soon as flour begins to brown; continue basting every fifteen minutes until meat is done, which will require about two hours; add one cup of stock to pan while meat is cooking. When richly browned cover closely and finish cooking.

To carve a boned leg of lamb, cut in thin slices across the grain, beginning at top of shoulder. When trussed in shape meat looks like a goose without wings or legs.

STUFFING FOR LAMB

(See recipe Page 154 for stuffing, adding ¾ teaspoon poultry seasoning.)

MINT SAUCE

1 bunch of mint finely chopped.
$\frac{1}{3}$ cup vinegar.
2 tablespoons cold water.
2 tablespoons powdered sugar.

PROCESS: Dilute vinegar with cold water, add sugar and stir until sugar is dissolved, pour over mint (there should be four tablespoons of mint), place on back of range and infuse for one-half hour.

NEW POTATOES WITH NEW PEAS

Prepare potatoes as for New Potatoes with Chive Sauce (see recipe Page 78), omitting the Chives. Cook one cup of new peas until tender, in as little boiling salted water as possible. Drain; add to potatoes. Reheat potatoes and peas in Cream Sauce.

SWISS CHARD WITH BACON

Wash and pick over Swiss Chard. Cook in boiling salted water, using just enough water to prevent Chard from burning. Drain and chop fine. Arrange in a mound on a chop platter, surround (crown fashion) with "hard-boiled" eggs cut in halves lengthwise, having cut side out. Cut a slice off the large end of each egg so that they will stay in place. Cut five slices of bacon in narrow strips crosswise. Try out one-third cup. Add one-fourth cup vinegar, diluted with one-fourth cup hot water, pour while hot over the Swiss Chard, scattering the scraps of bacon over top of mound.

CHERRY DUFF

4 cups pitted cherries.
2 cups sugar.
1 teaspoon lemon juice.
1½ tablespoons Cottolene.
2 cups flour.
4 teaspoons baking powder.
1 teaspoon salt.
¾ cup milk or thin cream.

Process: Mix and sift flour, baking powder and salt; rub Cottolene in lightly with the tips of fingers; add milk and mix to soft dough. Put sugar, cherries, drained from juice, and lemon juice in bottom of well-greased baking dish. Cover with dough, place in steamer, set over kettle of boiling water, lay a crash towel over steamer, replace cover, and steam pudding forty-five minutes. Serve with cherry juice, thickened with arrow root and sweetened.

I'm quite ashamed—'tis mighty rude
To eat so much—but all's so good!

#

Cold Consommé

Veal Loaf (Hot)—Tomato Sauce

(or)

Cold—with String Bean Salad

Saratoga Chips   Beets in Drawn Butter

Figs in Sherry Jelly with Whipped Cream

Nut and Raisin Cake with Caramel Frosting

Iced Coffee

CHICKEN CONSOMMÉ (COLD)

Place a four-pound fowl in stock pot and a small knuckle of veal; add four quarts of cold water and heat slowly to boiling point. Skim, reduce heat and let simmer five hours. Do not allow liquid to boil as it will destroy its gelatinous properties, and the stock will be turbid. The last hour of cooking add one-third cup each celery, carrot and turnip cut in small dice, one-third cup sliced onion, one teaspoon peppercorns, one tablespoon salt, three sprays thyme, one spray marjoram, two sprays parsley, one-half bay leaf. Remove fowl and knuckle; strain soup through double cheese cloth, cool quickly, and remove all fat; clear. Fill Bouillon cups three-fourths full and chill. This should be a clear, savory jelly.

TO CLEAR SOUP STOCK

After straining the stock through double cheese cloth, remove all fat and put the stock into a four-quart stew-pan. Place on range and allow the white and shell of one egg for each quart of stock. Beat the eggs slightly and crush shells in small bits, add slowly to stock, stirring constantly but slowly until the boiling point is reached; let boil two minutes. Reduce the heat so that stock barely simmers twenty minutes, skim and strain through double cheese cloth placed over fine soup strainer. If stock to be cleared is not sufficiently seasoned, add more seasoning before clearing.

VEAL LOAF

Wipe three pounds of lean veal, discarding all skin and tissue. Pass meat through the meat-chopper twice, with one-half pound of salt pork; add six crackers rolled, one-fourth cup cream, juice of one small lemon (about two tablespoons), one tablespoon salt, one-half tablespoon black pepper, onion juice to taste. Mix thoroughly and pack solidly in a granite, brick-shaped bread pan, spread top evenly and brush with slightly beaten white of egg. Bake in a moderate oven three hours, basting often with one-fourth cup of pork fat or dripping diluted with one-fourth cup boiling water. Prick surface with a fork that fat may penetrate meat. Chill, remove to serving platter, surround by any good vegetable salad. If served hot, surround with Tomato, Creole or Espagnole Sauce. This may be prepared Saturday.

STRING BEAN SALAD

Marinate cold, cooked, stringless beans with French Dressing. There should be enough beans to make a generous border around a cold veal loaf. Sprinkle beans thickly with small onions thinly sliced and the rings separated. Garnish edge of dish with sprays of parsley and Nasturtium blossoms. The finely chopped seed-cells may also be sprinkled over beans and is quite an addition.

SARATOGA CHIPS

Wash and pare the desired number of uniform-sized potatoes. Slice thinly (using slaw cutter) into a bowl of cold water. Let stand several hours, changing the water often or until it is quite clear. Drain and drop them into a kettle of boiling water; allow them to boil just one minute. Drain quickly and cover with cold water. Drain from cold water and dry between towels. Fry a few at a time in deep hot Cottolene, keeping them moving with the skimmer. Drain on soft brown paper and sprinkle with salt.

BEETS IN DRAWN BUTTER

Wash the small new beets and cook in boiling salted water until tender. Drain and cover with cold water. Rub off the skins and slice them or cut them in cubes. Reheat them in

DRAWN BUTTER (SOUR SAUCE)

Melt two tablespoons butter in a sauce-pan; add three tablespoons flour, stir to a smooth paste and add gradually, while stirring constantly, one cup boiling water. Boil two minutes, then add four tablespoons hot cream and four tablespoons vinegar (if vinegar is too acid use two tablespoons each of vinegar and water), season with salt and pepper.

FIGS IN SHERRY JELLY

1 tablespoon granulated gelatine.
¼ cup cold water.
¾ cup boiling water.
½ cup best table Sherry wine.
Juice of 1 small lemon.
½ dozen washed figs.
Whipped Cream.
½ cup sugar.

PROCESS: Soak gelatine in cold water, then dissolve it in boiling water; add sugar and stir occasionally until mixture begins to thicken, then add wine and lemon juice. Chill a pint mold in ice water (a fancy mold is attractive for this purpose). Separate the figs, slice them thinly and dip some of them in the jelly and use them for decorating the mold; then fill the mold with alternate layers of sliced figs and the mixture, allowing the jelly to "set" each time before adding the slices of figs. Chill thoroughly. Unmold jelly on serving dish and surround with whipped cream sweetened and flavored as desired. Use pastry bag and rose tube for this purpose.

NUT AND RAISIN CAKE

⅓ cup Cottolene.
1 cup fine sugar.
3 eggs unbeaten.
1 cup pecan nut meats.
⅔ cup raisins.
2 cups pastry flour.
4 teaspoons baking powder.
¾ cup milk.
Grated rind of half an orange.
½ teaspoon cinnamon.
¼ teaspoon mace.
¼ teaspoon salt.

PROCESS: Cream Cottolene, add sugar gradually, stirring constantly, add eggs, one at a time and beating each in thoroughly before adding another. Pass nuts and raisins through meat chopper, then mix with flour sifted with baking powder, salt and spices; add alternately to first mixture with milk, beating constantly. Turn mixture into a well-greased tube pan and bake thirty-five to forty minutes in a moderate oven. Spread with

CARAMEL FROSTING WITH NUTS

1¼ cups soft brown sugar.
¼ cup granulated sugar.
½ cup boiling water.
Whites 2 eggs.
½ teaspoon almond extract.
½ cup pecan nut meats broken in pieces.

PROCESS: Boil sugar and water together as for Boiled Frosting (see recipe Page 56). Pour slowly onto beaten whites of eggs, beating constantly, continue beating until frosting is nearly cool. Put pan containing frosting in a larger vessel of boiling water, place on range and cook until mixture granulates around sides of pan, stir constantly while cooking. Remove from hot water and beat until frosting will keep its shape when dropped from spoon. Add nut meats and flavoring. Spread on cake, using wooden spoon to give surface a wave-like appearance.

Menu
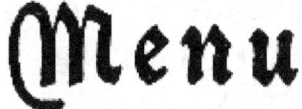

Consommé with Vegetables

Baked Stuffed Black Bass—Egg Sauce

Parsley Potatoes   Cauliflower with Cheese Sauce

Thin Corn Bread

Tomato and Onion Salad

Steamed Blueberry Pudding—Foamy Sauce

Iced Tea   Café Noir

CONSOMMÉ WITH VEGETABLES

To six cups Consommé (for recipe see Page 149) add French string beans cut in diamonds, carrots cooked and cut in tiny fancy shapes (using French vegetable cutters), and French peas. Serve with toasted Cheese Crackers.

BAKED BLACK BASS

Clean a four-pound Black Bass, pickerel or haddock, sprinkle with salt, stuff and sew with No. 8 cotton thread. Cut four or five diagonal gashes on each side of backbone and lay in strips of fat salt pork. Have the gashes on one side come between gashes on the other. The fish may be skewered in the shape of the letter S, or placed in an upright position on a well-greased fish sheet, laid in the bottom of a dripping-pan. Brush over with melted butter and sprinkle with salt and pepper, dredge with flour and strew small pieces of fat pork around fish. Bake one hour in a hot oven, basting every ten minutes, first with melted butter or dripping, then with fat in dripping-pan as it is tried out. Dispose on hot serving platter, pour around Egg Sauce and garnish with sprays of parsley.

STUFFING FOR FISH

½ cup cracker crumbs.
1 cup stale bread crumbs.
5 tablespoons butter.
½ teaspoon salt.
$\frac{1}{8}$ teaspoon pepper.
½ cup hot water.
Onion juice.

PROCESS: Mix crumbs, add seasoning, melt butter and hot water, add to crumbs, toss lightly with a fork and add onion juice to taste.

EGG SAUCE

To Drawn Butter Sauce add one-half teaspoon Anchovy Essence and two hard-cooked eggs cut in thin slices. Sprinkle all with finely chopped parsley. (For Drawn Butter Sauce see Page 92.)

THIN CORN BREAD

¾ cup yellow corn meal.
1¼ cups flour.
2 tablespoons sugar.
5 teaspoons baking powder.
¾ teaspoon salt.
1 cup thin cream.
1 egg well beaten.
2 tablespoons Cottolene.

PROCESS: Mix and sift the dry ingredients; add cream, beaten egg and Cottolene, beat thoroughly; bake in a well-greased, shallow pan, in a hot oven, twenty-five minutes; five minutes before removing from oven, brush over with melted butter or milk to give it a richer color. Serve with baked or broiled fish.

PARSLEY POTATOES

Select smooth, uniform-sized new potatoes; wash, scrape and cover with cold water. Let stand one hour; drain and place in steamer, cover closely and steam until soft. Remove to serving dish; dot over with bits of butter and sprinkle at once with coarse salt and finely chopped parsley.

CAULIFLOWER WITH CHEESE SAUCE

Select a medium-sized, firm cauliflower. Trim off leaves, cut off stalk, and soak one hour (head down) in cold salt water to cover. Cook (head up) until soft but not broken (about thirty minutes) in boiling salted water. Drain and place carefully in a buttered, shallow baking dish, pour over one and one-half cups of Cheese Sauce, sprinkle with buttered crumbs and place in oven until crumbs are browned. Serve in baking dish.

CHEESE SAUCE

3 tablespoons butter.
2 tablespoons flour.
½ teaspoon salt.
$1/8$ teaspoon pepper.
Few grains cayenne.
1½ cups hot milk.
½ cup cheese cut in small pieces.

PROCESS: Melt butter in a sauce-pan, add flour, mixed with seasonings, stir to a smooth paste; let cook one minute, stirring constantly. Pour on gradually hot milk and beat until smooth and glossy. Add cheese and when melted pour over cauliflower.

TOMATO AND ONION SALAD

Arrange a nest of heart lettuce leaves in salad bowl; place in center three peeled and chilled tomatoes, cut in quarters; thinly slice a mild onion, separate the rings and strew them over tomatoes, sprinkle all with green and red peppers finely chopped. Serve with French Dressing.

STEAMED BLUEBERRY PUDDING

2⅛ cups bread flour.
4 teaspoons baking powder.
1 teaspoon salt.
2 tablespoons Cottolene.
1 cup milk.
1 cup blueberries.

PROCESS: Mix and sift flour, baking powder and salt; rub in Cottolene with tips of fingers, add milk gradually, stirring constantly; turn on a floured board, knead slightly, then roll out to one-half inch thickness; place berries in center mixed with one-half teaspoon salt and two tablespoons sugar; fold dough over, pinch the edges together to form a large ball; lift carefully into a well-greased, two-quart pail, cover closely and steam one and one-half hours. Serve with

FOAMY SAUCE

2 egg whites.
1 cup sugar.
¾ cup thin hot cream.
1 tablespoon Sherry Wine.
Nutmeg.

PROCESS: Beat the whites of eggs until stiff, add sugar gradually, beating constantly. Add hot cream slowly, continue beating. Add Sherry wine and a sprinkle of nutmeg. Milk may be used in place of cream, if the latter is not available.

July
Third Sunday

Fifty-Two Sunday Dinners

#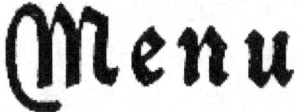

Tomato Bouillon—Cheesed Butter Thins

Radishes   Pickles

Cold Boiled Tongue   Chili Sauce

Potato Salad—Broiled Tomatoes

Blueberry Pie—Cheese Balls

Iced Café au Lait

Iced Cocoa

TOMATO BOUILLON

Prepare a tomato sauce; there should be two cups. Strain this while hot through one thickness of cheese cloth into six cups of hot Bouillon. Reheat and serve in Bouillon cups with

CHEESED BUTTER THINS

Sprinkle Butter Thins lightly with grated cheese, seasoned with salt and a few grains cayenne. Place in the oven until crackers are crisp and cheese is melted.

BOILED TONGUE

Wash and clean the tongue, cover with boiling water, to which add one-third cup each carrots, turnips and onion cut in dice; two sprays each

A Book of Recipes

parsley and thyme, one-half teaspoon peppercorns and one-half dozen cloves. Simmer until tongue is tender. Let cool in liquor in which it was cooked, remove the skin and brush with melted butter. Cover with fine, buttered bread crumbs, after arranging in dripping pan. Bake twenty minutes, basting often with hot stock or port wine. Chill and slice thinly; garnish with triangles of buttered toast sprinkled with finely chopped parsley.

CHILI SAUCE

2 dozen ripe tomatoes.
1 dozen onions finely chopped.
1 dozen peppers finely chopped.
1 cup brown sugar.
4 cups cider vinegar.
4 tablespoons salt.

PROCESS: Scald, peel and chop tomatoes; then add remaining ingredients in the order given. Place on range, bring to boiling point and cook slowly until thick. Add more salt and sugar if necessary. Turn into sterilized fruit jars, seal and store. Serve with meats, fish, etc.

POTATO SALAD

Cut balls from raw potatoes, using a French vegetable cutter. There should be three cups. Cook potato balls with three slices of onion in boiling salted water until tender. Drain, chill and marinate with French Dressing, then cover with Boiled Dressing. Arrange in a mound on serving platter, surrounded with a border of nasturtium blossoms and leaves. Sprinkle top with finely chopped chives.

BOILED SALAD DRESSING

¼ cup butter.
1¼ teaspoons salt.
1 teaspoon mustard.
¼ teaspoon paprika.
1 tablespoon sugar.
Yolks 4 eggs.
2 tablespoons flour.

¼ cup vinegar diluted with 2 tablespoons water.
1 cup cream.

Process: Melt butter in sauce-pan; add flour mixed with seasonings, add egg yolks slightly beaten and vinegar and water. Cook over hot water until mixture thickens. Cool. Whip cream and fold into mixture. Beat well, chill and serve with potato salad.

BROILED TOMATOES

Cut firm, ripe tomatoes in halves, crosswise. Rub each half lightly with a clove of garlic, sprinkle with salt, pepper, and fine, buttered bread crumbs mixed with a tablespoon of sugar. Place in a well-buttered broiler and broil five minutes. Remove carefully to a well-buttered shallow ramekin, dot over with bits of butter, finish cooking in the oven, and serve.

BLUEBERRY PIE

Line a deep, perforated pie tin with Plain Paste; brush over with white of egg slightly beaten. Fill with three cups blueberries mixed with one cup sugar, two tablespoons flour, one tablespoon butter cut in bits, one-eighth teaspoon salt, one tablespoon lemon juice. Wet edges, cover with crust, flute the rim and bake thirty-five minutes in a hot oven at first to set the crust, then reduce the heat and finish baking.

CHEESE BALLS

Rub to a paste one roll Neufchatel cheese; to this add one-half cup chopped pecan meats and one-half teaspoon finely chopped, mild red pepper; season with salt and roll with the "butter paddles" in small balls the size of Queen olives. Serve with berry or cherry pies.

ICED CAFÉ AU LAIT

1 cup medium ground coffee.
White 1 egg.
3 cups boiling water.
3 cups scalded milk.
1 cup cold water.

Process: Scald enameled coffee pot. Beat white of egg slightly. Dilute with one-half cup cold water, mix with coffee, turn into coffee pot and add boiling water, stir until well mixed. Place on range and let boil five minutes. Stir down and pour some into a cup to clear the spout of grounds. Return to pot and add remaining half cup of cold water. Place on back of range for ten minutes, where it will keep hot but not boil. After removing coffee to back of range, put milk into double boiler and, when scalded, pour the two together in another scalded coffee pot. Chill and serve.

July
Fourth Sunday

Fifty-Two Sunday Dinners

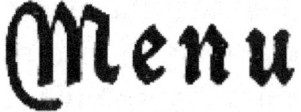

WATERMELON WITH SHERRY SAUCE

CONSOMMÉ PRINTANIERE—IMPERIAL RINGS

STUFFED HEARTS WITH VEGETABLES

POTATO PUFF

CABBAGE SALAD

RASPBERRY WHIP—WHITE NUT CAKE

ICED COFFEE

WATERMELON WITH SHERRY SAUCE

Scoop balls out of the center of watermelon using French potato cutter. Pour over Sherry Sauce and place them carefully in a freezer, packed in salt and ice, let stand until thoroughly chilled (about one and a half hours). Serve with Sherry Sauce in tall champagne glasses.

SHERRY SAUCE

Cook one cup sugar with one-fourth cup of water three minutes. Cool slightly and add one-half cup Sherry, three tablespoons Sloe gin and a sprinkle of salt. Chill and pour over watermelon balls.

CONSOMMÉ PRINTANIERE

A Book of Recipes

To one quart of Chicken Consommé add one tablespoon each of cooked carrot and turnip, cut in small fancy shapes (using French vegetable cutter for this purpose), small peas, French beans and asparagus tips. Heat these vegetables in a small quantity of hot consommé; drain, place them in hot soup tureen and pour over boiling consommé.

IMPERIAL RINGS

Cut stale bread in one-third inch slices. Stamp out circles three inches in diameter; with a smaller cutter (size of top of pepper shaker) cut out center, leaving rings about one-third inch wide. Brush with melted butter, sprinkle lightly with salt and paprika, and brown delicately in the oven. Serve in a circle overlapping each other on a plate covered with a doily.

STUFFED HEARTS WITH VEGETABLES

Clean and wash three calves' hearts; stuff and skewer into shape. Draw small strips of salt pork (lardoons) through edges of hearts. Sprinkle with salt and pepper, dredge with flour and brown well in hot Cottolene, with two slices onion, four slices carrot, one blade celery cut fine, two sprays parsley, two small bits bay leaf, three cloves and one-half teaspoon peppercorns. When hearts are richly browned, remove to Dutch oven, casserole or deep baking dish. Add two cups Brown Stock, cover closely and cook slowly in the oven until tender (about two hours), basting six times while cooking.

Cut three slices of stale bread one-third inch thick, shape with large round cutter; with a small cutter remove centers to form rings: brush with melted butter and brown delicately in the oven. Arrange them on hot serving platter, set a heart in each ring and surround with new carrots and turnips cut Julienne style and cooked in boiling salted water until tender. There should be one and one-half cups each. Drain and dress with Maître d'Hôtel Butter.

STUFFING FOR HEARTS
½ cup cracker crumbs.
½ cup stale bread crumbs.
2 inch cube fat salt pork finely chopped.
2 blades celery finely chopped.

½ teaspoon finely chopped parsley.
1 tablespoon onion finely chopped.
Salt, pepper.

Process: Mix ingredients in the order given and season well with salt and pepper.

POTATO PUFF

Prepare two and one-half cups hot mashed potatoes. Add two and one-half tablespoons butter, one-half teaspoon baking powder, season with salt and pepper and moisten with one-half cup hot cream or milk, beat thoroughly. Add the whites of two eggs beaten until stiff. Pile lightly in a buttered baking dish and bake until well puffed and browned.

NEW CABBAGE SALAD

Mix two cups of new cabbage, finely shredded, with one-half cup of celery cut in small pieces and one mild onion finely chopped. Add one-half tablespoon Worcestershire Sauce to one cup of boiled salad dressing and mix thoroughly with cabbage. Chill. Serve in onion cups or in nests of crisp lettuce leaves.

RASPBERRY WHIP

1½ cups red raspberries.
1 cup powdered sugar.
White 1 egg.

Process: Mix sugar with berries and turn into bowl in which white of egg is slightly beaten, then mash berries and sugar and mix thoroughly with egg. Beat with a wire whip until mixture is stiff to stand. Pile lightly on a chilled serving dish and surround with macaroons. Serve with

GOLDEN SAUCE

1 egg.
1 cup powdered sugar.
3 tablespoons Sherry wine.

PROCESS: Beat yolks until thick and light, add one half the sugar gradually, beating constantly: beat whites until stiff, gradually adding the remaining half cup sugar. Combine mixtures, add wine and beat thoroughly.

WHITE NUT CAKE

1/3 cup Cottolene.
1½ cups fine sugar.
¾ cup cold water.
2¼ cups pastry flour.
4 teaspoons baking powder.
¼ teaspoon salt.
Whites 4 eggs beaten until stiff.
½ teaspoon Almond extract.
1 cup English walnut meats broken in pieces.

PROCESS: Cream Cottolene, add sugar gradually, beating constantly. Mix and sift flour, baking powder and salt, add alternately to first mixture with water, add nut meats and extract; cut and fold in whites of eggs. Bake in a sheet thirty-five minutes in a moderate oven. Spread with

MAPLE FROSTING

1 cup maple sugar.
½ cup boiling water.
White 1 egg.
1/8 teaspoon cream of tartar.

PROCESS: Boil sugar, water and cream of tartar together until it spins a thread from tip of spoon. Pour slowly in a fine stream on the beaten white and continue beating until of the consistency to spread over cake. (To get the exact proportion of sugar, weigh one level cup of granulated sugar to ascertain by weight how much Maple sugar is required for this amount of water and white of one egg. It will weigh about one-half pound.)

Fifty-Two Sunday Dinners

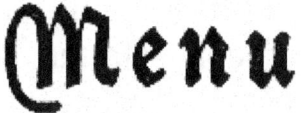

Menu

Cream of Lettuce Soup

Pressed Chicken   Tomato Salad

Lattice Potatoes—Green Corn Pudding

Peach Ice Cream—Rich Chocolate Cake

Spiced Iced Tea

CREAM OF LETTUCE SOUP
2 cups White Stock.
2 heads lettuce.
2 tablespoons rice.
2 tablespoons butter.
1 teaspoon finely chopped onion.
½ cup hot cream.
1 egg yolk.
Salt and pepper.
Few grains nutmeg.

Process: Cook the onion in butter five minutes (without browning), add rice, lettuce finely chopped, and stock, cover and cook until rice is soft; add hot cream, slightly beaten yolk of egg and seasonings. Do not allow soup to boil after adding egg yolk. Discard outer leaves of lettuce, using only the hearts for soup.

PRESSED CHICKEN

A Book of Recipes

Disjoint a four- or five-pound fowl, cover with boiling water and let simmer until tender, with one carrot sliced, one onion sliced, a blade or two of celery broken in inch pieces, two sprays parsley and one-half teaspoon peppercorns. Add one tablespoon salt the last hour of cooking. Drain chicken from liquor, remove the skin and bones; strain liquor, return to range and let simmer until reduced to one cup, strain and reserve. When the meat is nearly cold, cut it in small cubes or chop fine; remove all fat from liquor, reheat and add chicken, stirring it slowly, season with salt and pepper if necessary. Decorate a granite, brick-shaped bread pan with "hard boiled" eggs cut in rings or fancy shapes, over these pack the chicken mixture very carefully so as not to disturb the decorations. Cover with a buttered paper, place a weight over paper and let stand over night in a cold place. Serve with Tomato Salad.

TOMATO SALAD

Wash garden cress and shake dry, arrange a bed on large oval platter, discarding all coarse leaves and stems. Peel and chill five uniform-sized tomatoes, cut a slice from the stem ends and scoop out the pulp, invert tomato cups on a plate and set aside in a cool place. Chop fine the solid pulp of the tomato with one chilled and pared cucumber, add two tablespoons finely chopped chives, stir in one cup of Cream Dressing and refill tomato cups with mixture heaping them in pyramids. Dispose these tomato cups at intervals in cress border and place mold of pressed chicken in center.

CREAM SALAD DRESSING

1½ teaspoon salt.
½ tablespoon mustard.
1 tablespoon sugar.
1 egg slightly beaten.
2½ tablespoons melted butter.
¾ cup cream.
4 tablespoons vinegar.

PROCESS: Mix ingredients in the order given, adding vinegar very slowly, beating constantly. Cook in double boiler until mixture thickens; continue beating, strain at once and chill.

LATTICE POTATOES

Wash and pare potatoes of a uniform size. Slice on a corrugated vegetable slicer, which is made for this purpose. Wash slices in cold water, changing the water several times; then let stand several hours in cold water. Drain and dry with crash towels. Fry a few at a time in deep hot Cottolene, drain on brown paper, sprinkle with salt. Pile on a lace paper doily in a fancy basket.

GREEN CORN PUDDING

To two cups of cooked green corn, cut from the cob (or one can of corn) chopped fine, add two eggs slightly beaten, one teaspoon salt, one-eighth teaspoon pepper, one teaspoon sugar, two tablespoons melted butter, and two cups scalded milk. Mix well and turn into a buttered pudding dish; bake until firm in moderate oven.

PEACH ICE CREAM NO. 1

1½ cups peach pulp.
1½ cups granulated sugar.
Juice one lemon.
1 quart thin cream.

PROCESS: Pare and stone choice, ripe peaches and rub the pulp through a purée strainer; add sugar and lemon juice, turn into the can of freezer packed in ice and salt (using three measures of crushed ice to one of rock salt); add cream and freeze in the usual way.

RICH CHOCOLATE CAKE

½ cup Cottolene.
1½ cups sugar.
4 eggs.
4 squares chocolate.
1 teaspoon cinnamon.
⅓ cup hot water.
½ cup milk.
2 cups flour.
3 teaspoons baking powder.
¼ teaspoon salt.
1 teaspoon vanilla.

PROCESS: Cream Cottolene, add sugar gradually, stirring constantly. Melt chocolate over hot water, add hot water specified in recipe and beat immediately into creamed butter and sugar; add yolks of eggs beaten until thick and light. Mix and sift flour, cinnamon, baking powder and salt; add to first mixture alternately with milk, add vanilla. Cut and fold in the stiffly-beaten whites of eggs. Bake in a shallow pan forty to forty-five minutes. Cover with Boiled Frosting (for recipe see Page 56).

SPICED ICED TEA

4 teaspoons tea.
2 cups boiling water.
9 cloves.

PROCESS: Follow recipe for making tea. Strain into pitcher over cloves, chill, then pour into glasses filled with cracked ice. Sweeten to taste. The flavor of tea is preserved and is much finer by chilling the infusion quickly, before pouring over ice. Allow three cloves for each glass. The large Penang cloves are the best.

Menu

Nova Scotia Canapés

Pan Broiled Fillets of Beef—Sultana Sauce

Carlsbad Potatoes   Peas and Onions French Style

Lettuce, Peppergrass and Onion Salad

Peach Ice Cream—Cocoanut Cake

Coffee

NOVA SCOTIA CANAPÉS

Cut white bread in one-third inch slices; stamp out with heart-shaped cutter; spread both sides thinly with butter, brown them delicately in the oven. Mince Nova Scotia smoked salmon and moisten with Mayonnaise or Boiled Salad Dressing. Spread each heart with mixture, dispose a dainty border of finely chopped white of egg around each and tip it off with a sprinkle of the yolk pressed through a sieve. Do not cover the salmon entirely with the egg. Arrange canapés on small plates covered with a lace paper doily; garnish each with a spray of parsley and serve as first course.

PAN BROILED FILLETS OF BEEF

Have fillets of beef cut one and one-half inches thick; shape in circular forms. Broil ten minutes in a hissing, well-buttered frying pan, turning every ten seconds for the first two minutes, that the surface may be seared thoroughly, thus preventing the loss of juices. Turn occasionally afterward.

When half done season with salt, pepper, reduce heat and finish cooking. Arrange on hot serving platter and spread generously with soft butter. Pour over Sultana Sauce. (For recipe see Page 61.)

CARLSBAD POTATOES

Wash and pare one dozen small, uniform-sized potatoes; soak one hour in cold water to cover. Drain, put in stew-pan and cover with one quart of boiling water. Add two tablespoons butter and two teaspoons salt. Cook until soft (but not broken), then drain. Return to stew-pan. Add one-third cup butter, one and one-half tablespoons lemon juice, and one-eighth teaspoon paprika. Cook four or five minutes, shaking the pan occasionally. Place in hot serving dish and sprinkle with one tablespoon chopped parsley.

PEAS AND ONIONS—FRENCH STYLE

Cut one slice bacon in shreds crosswise, using the shears for this purpose. Cook bacon with one-fourth cup butter about ten minutes, without scorching bacon. Remove scraps of bacon, add two cups fresh peas, one dozen small onions and a sprig of mint. Cook until peas and onions are soft, adding one-fourth cup boiling water to prevent scorching. Beat one egg yolk slightly, add one-third cup cream and one head of lettuce cut in quarters (use lettuce hearts), season with salt and pepper. Let boil up once and serve.

LETTUCE, PEPPERGRASS AND ONION SALAD

Separate the heart leaves of two solid heads of lettuce. Wash, drain and chill; arrange them in a nest in salad bowl. Sprinkle between and over leaves four tablespoons finely chopped peppergrass and small, thinly sliced onions, separating the rings. Marinate with French Dressing; chill and serve.

PEACH ICE CREAM No. 2
    4 cups milk.
    3 cups heavy cream.
    1 cup sugar.
    1 tablespoon lemon extract.

¼ teaspoon salt.
2 cups fresh peach pulp.

Process: Pare and pit peaches; stew until soft, rub through a sieve. Then mix ingredients in the order given. Add peach pulp and freeze. Let stand two hours before serving.

COCOANUT CAKE

(For recipe see Page 56.)

August
Second Sunday

Fifty-Two Sunday Dinners

Menu

Consommé (Cold)

Broiled Chicken—Sauce Viennaise

Potato Roses   Corn Fritters

Cauliflower à la Béchamel

Dressed Head Lettuce

Salad Rolls

Blackberry Roly-Poly   Creamy Sauce

Coffee

COLD CONSOMMÉ

(For recipe see Page 90.)

BROILED CHICKEN

Singe, wipe and with a sharp pointed knife (a boning knife) split the broiler down the back the entire length, beginning at back of neck. Lay open and remove entrails, etc., remove ribs and breast-bone, then cut the tendons at joints. Rub bird over with soft butter, sprinkle with salt and place on a well-greased broiler or in a well-greased wire broiler. Cook twenty-five minutes under a gas flame or over glowing coals, turning often. Baste bird over several times with melted butter if it appears dry. When evenly

A Book of Recipes

browned, remove to well-greased dripping pan, spread again with soft butter, cover closely, and bake until tender at the joints. Serve with

SAUCE VIENNAISE

Reduce one small can of tomatoes by slow cooking to a thick pulp; when strained there should be two tablespoons. To three-fourths cup Mayonnaise Dressing add three-fourths tablespoon finely chopped capers, one teaspoon finely chopped parsley, two teaspoons each finely chopped gherkins and olives, one teaspoon finely chopped onion or chives. Add tomato pulp, mix well and keep in a cool place until ready to serve.

MASHED POTATOES (FOR ROSES)

To three cups of hot riced potatoes add three tablespoons butter, one teaspoon salt, the beaten yolks of three eggs and enough hot milk to allow the mixture to pass readily through the pastry-bag with rose tube attached. Shape as roses on a buttered tin sheet, brush over lightly with egg slightly beaten and diluted with one tablespoon milk, and brown delicately in oven.

To Shape Roses

Fill pastry bag with potato mixture. Hold the bag upright with tube pointing downward. Guide tube with left hand and press out potato with the right, making a circular motion. When roses are the desired size press the tube gently into mixture and withdraw it quickly to stop the flow and give the pyramid a pointed finish. Sweet potatoes may be prepared in the same manner.

CORN FRITTERS

(For recipe see Page 63.)

CAULIFLOWER À LA BÉCHAMEL

Select a firm, white cauliflower, remove leaves and cut off the stalk. Soak (head down) in cold salt water to cover. Drain and cook (head up) in boiling salted water to cover until tender but not broken apart. Drain well and dispose on shallow serving dish. Pour over one and one-half cups Béchamel Sauce (see Page 85). Sprinkle with finely chopped parsley.

DRESSED HEAD LETTUCE

Select a large, firm head of lettuce. Remove all wilted leaves. Separate the heart leaves sufficiently to wash them thoroughly. Drain, arrange leaves on shallow serving plate, keeping them in their original shape if possible. Sprinkle over all finely shredded red and green prepared peppers. (To prepare peppers, plunge them into boiling water, then quickly rub off the glazed outer skin, drop peppers into cold water until crisp. Cut a slice from the stem ends, remove seeds and veins, then cut in thread like rings.) Serve with French Dressing, to which add one tablespoon Roquefort cheese. Blend well before pouring over Salad.

BLACKBERRY ROLY-POLY

2 cups blackberries.
¼ cup water.
1 cup sugar.
¼ teaspoon salt.
2 cups pastry flour.
4 teaspoons baking powder.
½ teaspoon salt.
4 tablespoons Cottolene.
Yolk 1 egg.
White 1 egg slightly beaten.
Granulated sugar.
Ground cloves.

PROCESS: Cook blackberries in water and salt until berries are soft. Rub through a sieve and add sugar to pulp; return to range and cook until mixture thickens, stirring occasionally. Sift flour with baking powder and salt, work in Cottolene with tips of fingers, and mix to a soft dough with yolk of egg mixed with one-half cup of milk. Turn onto a floured board, knead slightly and roll out in a rectangular sheet one-fourth inch thick. Divide this into four pieces, longer than wide. Spread each with the blackberry sauce and roll up like jelly roll; wet the edges, press lightly to prevent unrolling. Lay on buttered sheet and brush tops with white of egg, sprinkle with sugar and a few grains cloves. Bake twenty-five minutes in a hot oven. Serve hot with remaining sauce kept hot over hot water or with

##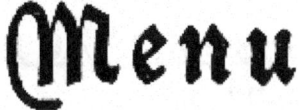

CANTALOUPE À LA MODE

CONSOMMÉ AU RIZ—CHEESE BALLS

SPICED BEEF—WHIPPED CREAM HORSERADISH SAUCE

POTATOES ITALIAN STYLE—SUCCOTASH

PEAR SALAD

PEACH COTTAGE PUDDING WITH CREAM

COFFEE

CANTALOUPE À LA MODE

Wash small ripe cantaloupe (Rockyfords) with a brush, and chill thoroughly. Cut in halves lengthwise and fill with Pineapple or Raspberry Ice. Arrange on a bed of cracked ice; serve one-half melon to each guest.

RASPBERRY ICE

4 cups water.
1-¾ cups sugar.
2 cups raspberry pulp.
¼ cup orange juice.
2 tablespoons lemon juice.

PROCESS: Make a syrup by boiling water and sugar twenty minutes. Mash berries and rub through a fine sieve, add orange and lemon juice, combine with syrup, strain and freeze. Shape with a cone mold and place in seed cavities of halves of cantaloupe.

CONSOMMÉ AU RIZ

8 cups consommé.
¼ cup washed rice.
6 cups cold water.
½ tablespoon salt.

PROCESS: Add salt to boiling water, then add rice slowly and let cook until rice is soft; drain. Pour over rice six cups cold water to separate kernels. Add rice to hot consommé and serve with Cheese Balls.

CHEESE BALLS

4 tablespoons butter.
¾ cup flour.
½ cup water.
¼ teaspoon salt.
Few grains cayenne.
3 eggs.
¼ cup grated Edam Cheese.
Cottolene.

PROCESS: Melt butter in a sauce-pan, add water, cook one minute; add flour mixed with seasonings. Cook until mixture leaves the sides of pan, stirring constantly. Cool slightly, add unbeaten eggs one at a time, add cheese. Mix well and drop from tip of teaspoon into deep hot Cottolene. Drain and serve immediately.

SPICED BEEF

Wash and wipe six pounds of beef cut from the flank. Cover with boiling water; bring to the boiling point and skim. Reduce heat and simmer until meat is tender (time required about five hours), adding the last hour of cooking one-half cup each of carrot, onion and celery cut in dice, two sprays each of parsley and thyme, one of marjoram, six cloves, one-half teaspoon peppercorns and one tablespoon salt. Remove meat and reduce liquor to one and one-half cups; strain. Shred the meat, mix with the liquor and press in a granite, brick-shaped bread pan, packing solidly. When thoroughly cold, serve, cut in thin slices, with Whipped Cream Horseradish Sauce (for recipe see [Page 120](#)).

POTATOES A L'ITALIENNE

To two cups hot riced potatoes, add one tablespoon finely chopped chives, one egg yolk well beaten, whites four eggs beaten until stiff, one-half cup grated cheese. Season with salt, pepper and a few grains cayenne. Pile lightly in a well-greased baking dish and bake from twenty-five to thirty minutes. Turn dish around several times carefully that mixture may puff evenly.

SUCCOTASH

Shell lima beans, wash and cover with boiling water; heat to boiling point and drain; throw away water and rinse beans, drain again. Cook in boiling, salted water until tender. Drain and add to an equal quantity of hot boiled corn cut from the cob. Season with salt, pepper and butter. Reheat before serving.

PEAR SALAD

Wipe, pare and remove the cores from the desired number of ripe (early) pears. Cut in eighths lengthwise. Arrange on beds of crisp cress, or lettuce heart leaves. Bestrew with prepared red peppers cut in very fine rings. Serve with French Dressing, using lemon juice in place of vinegar. Canned red peppers may be used when fresh peppers are not available. To prepare peppers, plunge them into boiling water for a moment, cut a slice from stem ends, remove seeds and veins, cover with cold water until crisp; drain dry, and cut in fine shreds.

PEACH COTTAGE PUDDING

¼ cup Cottolene.
1 cup sugar.
1 egg.
½ cup milk.
2 cups pastry flour.
4 teaspoons baking powder.
¼ teaspoon salt.

¼ teaspoon almond extract.
Fresh peaches sliced.

Process: Cream Cottolene, add sugar gradually, stirring constantly; add egg well beaten. Mix and sift flour, baking powder and salt; add to first mixture alternately with milk. Add extract and beat thoroughly. Turn into a well-greased shallow pan, and bake twenty-five minutes in a moderate oven. Cut in three-inch squares; pile thinly-sliced fresh peaches on top of each portion, sprinkle thickly with powdered sugar and serve with rich cream.

August
Fourth Sunday

#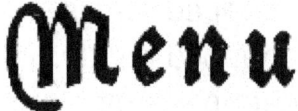

Boiled Halibut (Cold)—Vinaigrette Sauce

Cucumber Baskets   Radishes

French Fried Potatoes—Boiled Sweet Corn

Frozen Apricots—Sultana Cake

Demi Tasse

Iced Tea

BOILED HALIBUT—COLD

Have a piece of Halibut cut weighing two and one-half pounds. Tie in a square of cheese cloth (to prevent scum from settling on the flesh of fish). Cover with boiling water to which add salt and vinegar or lemon juice; the acid preserves the whiteness of the fish. Boil until the flesh leaves the bones (about thirty-five minutes). Drain and remove from cheese cloth. Pick out bones and remove skin. Place in a vessel that will preserve the shape of fish, chill and dispose fish on a cold serving platter on a bed of garden cress. Set a cucumber basket at intervals (one for each guest), and serve with

VINAIGRETTE SAUCE

1 teaspoon salt.
$1/8$ teaspoon black pepper.
Few grains cayenne.
1 tablespoon Tarragon vinegar.

2 tablespoons Malt vinegar.
½ cup Olive oil.
1 tablespoon chopped olives.
1 tablespoon chopped pickle.
1 tablespoon chopped green or red pepper.
1 teaspoon chopped parsley.
1½ teaspoons chopped chives.

PROCESS: Put salt, pepper and cayenne in bowl, add oil slowly stirring constantly, add remaining ingredients and blend thoroughly. Chill and pour over Boiled Halibut.

CUCUMBER BASKETS

Select long cucumbers of uniform thickness (three cucumbers will make six baskets), cut a slice from both the stem and blossom ends, pare and cut in halves crosswise; cut from each piece a section so as to form a handle crosswise of cucumber. Scoop out the soft pulp and seeds, brush each basket over lightly with olive oil and sprinkle with finely chopped garden cress or parsley. Fill the baskets with Mayonnaise Dressing or Sauce Tartare (see recipe Page 84). Chill and serve in nests of peppergrass or lettuce heart leaves.

FRENCH FRIED POTATOES

Wash and pare medium-sized potatoes, cut them lengthwise in eight pieces of a uniform size. Soak them in cold water two hours, changing the water several times. Drain from water and dry between towels. Then fry a few at a time in deep hot Cottolene. Drain on brown paper and sprinkle with salt. This is an easy method of preparing potatoes in hot weather. The potatoes may be prepared beforehand and the process of cooking is both simply and quickly done. Be sure the Cottolene is not too hot as the potatoes must be cooked through, as well as browned.

BOILED SWEET CORN

Have the water boiling. Remove the husks and silk from the corn and drop them at once into the boiling water; bring water quickly to boiling point and let boil rapidly five to ten minutes (depending somewhat on age of corn). Drain from water and arrange in a napkin-covered platter; serve at once.

FROZEN APRICOTS

Drain the apricots from the liquor in the can. Reserve liquor and cut fruit in one-fourth inch cubes. To the syrup add sufficient water to make four cups; add one cup orange juice; add one and one-half cups sugar. Cook five minutes, strain and pour over apricots; chill and freeze. Fresh apricots or peaches may be used when in season. The fresh fruit should be cooked until clear, in a syrup made of four cups of water and two cups sugar. When this mixture is frozen to a mush, two cups of Whipped Cream may be added, if one desires a richer dessert.

SULTANA CAKE

 ⅓ cup Cottolene.
 1 cup sugar.
 2 eggs.
 1 egg yolk.
 1 cup Sultana raisins.
 ½ cup milk.
 2¼ cups pastry flour.
 4 teaspoons baking powder.
 ¼ teaspoon salt.
 ½ teaspoon mace.

PROCESS: Cream Cottolene, add sugar gradually, stirring constantly; add well-beaten eggs and yolk. Mix and sift flour (except one tablespoon), baking powder and salt and mace; add to first mixture alternately with milk. Dredge raisins with tablespoon flour, add to mixture and beat thoroughly. Turn mixture into a well-greased, brick-shaped bread pan and bake forty minutes in a moderate oven. Frost if desired.

August
Fifth Sunday

Fifty-Two Sunday Dinners

#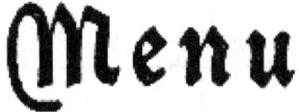

Tomato Canapé

Cold Veal Loaf—Whipped Cream Horseradish Sauce

Creamed New Potatoes   Steamed Summer Squash

Lettuce, Garden Cress and Onion Salad

Sliced Peaches—Chocolate Layer Cake

Iced Coffee   Lemonade

TOMATO CANAPÉ

Fry circles of bread, cut one-third inch thick, in deep hot Cottolene. Sauté slices of tomato in hot butter. Drain both on brown paper. Cover each circle of bread with a slice of tomato, sprinkle with salt, pepper and a few grains cayenne. Garnish each with a slice of cucumber and the white of "hard boiled" eggs, cut in the shape of petals to represent field daisies.

COLD VEAL LOAF

Have the bone of a knuckle of veal sawed in three pieces at the market. Wash, wipe, and put in kettle with two pounds of lean veal, one onion sliced, six slices carrot, one blade celery broken in pieces, one spray parsley and one-half teaspoon peppercorns; cover with boiling water and cook slowly until meat is tender. Drain; chop meat finely and season well with salt, pepper and a few grains cayenne. Reduce liquor to one cup, strain and reserve. Garnish the bottom of a granite, brick-shaped bread pan with the

A Book of Recipes

white of "hard boiled" egg cut to resemble three daisies; put a dot of the yolk in center of each and arrange sprays of parsley between each daisy. Put a layer of meat, then a layer of thinly sliced eggs sprinkled with parsley, finely chopped. Cover with remaining meat; pour over strained liquor, press and let stand until cold and jellied. Remove to serving platter, garnish with parsley and small round radishes cut to resemble tulips. Slice thinly and serve with

WHIPPED CREAM HORSERADISH SAUCE

    4 tablespoons freshly grated horseradish.
    Few drops onion juice.
    Few grains cayenne.
    1½ tablespoons vinegar.
    ¼ cup heavy cream whipped.
    ¼ teaspoon salt.

PROCESS: Mix the first five ingredients thoroughly, then fold in the whipped cream. Chill and serve.

CREAMED NEW POTATOES

Cut two and one-half cups cold, boiled new potatoes in one-half inch cubes. Add one and one-half cups White Sauce. Season highly with salt and white pepper, and reheat in double boiler. Remove to hot serving dish and sprinkle with finely chopped parsley.

STEAMED SUMMER SQUASH

Wash and cut in quarters. Cook in boiling salted water until tender. Drain through double cheese cloth. Pass through ricer or mash with potato masher, and season with butter, salt and a little black pepper. Reheat and serve.

LETTUCE, GARDEN CRESS AND ONION SALAD

Separate the crisp heart leaves of two heads of lettuce; arrange them on a shallow serving dish to represent a full-blown rose. Pick over, wash and dry a bunch of garden cress, chop finely and sprinkle over lettuce leaves. Chop one small onion very fine and mix with French dressing. Pour over lettuce. Serve at once.

SLICED PEACHES

Scald fine, ripe peaches; remove skins, cut in halves and remove stones. Slice lengthwise and arrange in serving dish in layers. Sprinkle each layer with sugar and lemon or orange juice. Chill and serve with cream and sugar.

The kitchen is a country in which there are always discoveries to be made.—La Reyniére.

Menu

Cream of Pea Soup—Crisp Saratoga Wafers

Braised Shoulder Veal Stuffed—Creole Sauce

Potato Balls   Spinach with Cream

Lettuce, Radish and Onion Salad

Apple Pie   Cottage Cheese

Café Noir

CREAM OF PEA SOUP

2 cups Marrowfat peas (or one can).
2 teaspoons sugar.
2 cups water.
1½ cups scalded milk.
1 slice onion.
1½ tablespoons butter.
2 tablespoons flour.
½ cup hot cream.
1 teaspoon salt.
$1/8$ teaspoon pepper.

Process: Peas that are too hard to serve as a vegetable may be used for soup. Cover them with the cold water and cook until soft. Rub through sieve, reheat pulp and thicken with butter and flour cooked together. Scald milk with onion, remove onion, add milk slowly to pea mixture, stirring constantly. Add hot cream and seasoning. Serve with Crisp Saratoga Wafers.

BRAISED SHOULDER OF VEAL

Have the bones removed from five pounds of the shoulder of veal (reserve bones). Stuff with bread stuffing, truss in shape and follow directions for Braised Beef (see Page 139). Add two sprays of thyme and marjoram. Serve with

CREOLE SAUCE

4 tablespoons Cottolene.
4 tablespoons flour.
¼ cup green pepper cut in shreds.
1 small clove garlic.
1 truffle cut in thin shreds.
1 can small button mushrooms.
1½ cups thick, well-seasoned tomato pulp.
1¼ cups Brown Stock.
Salt, pepper and cayenne.

Process: Cook pepper, onion and butter together five minutes without browning; add flour and cook two minutes, stirring constantly. Add truffle, tomato pulp and gradually Brown Stock; continue stirring until ingredients are well blended. Heat mushrooms in their own liquor, drain, and add mushrooms to sauce. Stick a tooth-pick through the clove of garlic, drop it into sauce and let it simmer fifteen minutes. Remove garlic before serving.

POTATO BALLS

Add to five hot mashed potatoes, one-fourth teaspoon celery salt, one teaspoon finely chopped parsley or chives, salt, pepper and three tablespoons butter, and enough hot milk to make of the consistency to handle. Shape into smooth, round balls, roll in flour, egg and crumbs. Fry a golden brown in deep, hot Cottolene. Dispose around Veal.

SPINACH WITH CREAM

Discard all wilted leaves, remove the roots and pick over and wash one-half peck of spinach in several waters, to rid it from all sand. If young and tender, put in a stew-pan and heat gradually; let boil twenty-five minutes, or until soft, in its own juices and the water that clung to the leaves. Old spinach should be cooked in boiling, salted water (it will require about two quarts of water to one peck spinach). Drain thoroughly, chop finely in a wooden bowl. Melt three tablespoons butter in an omelet pan; add spinach and cook four minutes, stirring constantly, sprinkle with one and one-half tablespoons flour, continue stirring and pour on gradually three-fourths cup hot, thin cream; simmer five minutes.

LETTUCE, RADISH AND ONION SALAD

Remove the leaves from the stalk, discarding all wilted and unsightly leaves. Wash and keep in cold water until crisp. Drain and dry on a crash towel or cheese cloth. Place between leaves thin slices of round, red radishes, sprinkle with finely sliced young green onions. Garnish with radishes cut to resemble tulips. Serve with French Dressing.

APPLE PIE

5 tart apples.
½ cup sugar.
¼ teaspoon nutmeg.
$\frac{1}{8}$ teaspoon salt.
1¼ tablespoons butter.
1 tablespoon lemon juice.
Grated rind ¼ lemon.

PROCESS: Line a pie pan with Plain Paste. Wipe, pare, core and cut apples in quarters, then in slices lengthwise. Pile them in lined pie pan, heaping them well in center, leaving a half-inch space around edge of pie. Mix sugar, nutmeg, salt, lemon juice, grated rind and turn over apples. Dot over with bits of butter; wet edges and cover with top crust; press and flute edges. Bake forty-five minutes in a moderate oven.

PLAIN PASTE

1½ cups flour.
½ teaspoon salt.

½ teaspoon baking powder.
¼ cup Cottolene.
Ice Water.

Process: Mix and sift flour, salt and baking powder. Rub in Cottolene (reserving one and one-half tablespoons), with tips of fingers. Add just enough ice water to form a soft dough, mixing it in with a knife. Turn on a floured board and roll out in a thin sheet, spread lightly with remaining Cottolene. Roll like jelly roll and cut in two pieces, having one piece a trifle larger than the other. Chill. Then stand rolls on end, press down with the hand and roll in circular piece to fit pie pan. The larger piece is for the top crust. This recipe makes the exact quantity of pastry for one medium-sized pie with two crusts. If desired, omit baking powder.

COTTAGE CHEESE

Put two quarts thick sour milk in a milk pan, place it on the back of range where it will not boil or simmer; allow it to remain there until the curd has separated from the whey. Lay a double square of cheese cloth over a bowl, turn in the milk, lift the edges and corners of cloth, draw them together, tie with a piece of twine and hang it up to drain. When quite dry, turn into a bowl; season with salt and mix with a silver fork, add sweet cream until of the desired consistency. Serve very cold with hot gingerbread.

September
Second Sunday

Fifty-Two Sunday Dinners

#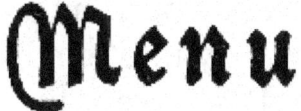

SUMMER SAUSAGE WITH

RIPE OLIVES AND DILL PICKLES

ROAST FILLET BEEF—MUSHROOM SAUCE

PARSLEY POTATOES   BROILED TOMATOES

BANANA FRITTERS

PEPPER AND ONION SALAD

MOCK MINCE PIE   CHEESE

ICED TEA

BUTTERMILK

SUMMER SAUSAGE (APPETIZER)

Cut summer sausage in very thin slices. Dispose them on a narrow platter overlapping one another. Garnish with sprays of peppergrass or parsley. Arrange thinly sliced dill pickles on either side of sausage, placing a ripe olive here and there; radishes cut to resemble roses may also be used. Serve as an appetizer.

ROAST FILLET OF BEEF

A Book of Recipes

Trim a small fillet of beef weighing about four pounds into shape. Lard the upper side and sprinkle with salt, pepper and dredge with flour. Sprinkle small cubes of fat salt pork thickly over the bottom of a dripping pan, set a wire trivet or rack on pork and lay meat on trivet. Place in a very hot oven at first, to sear over surface. Baste every five minutes for the first fifteen minutes, then several times after during the cooking. If liked rare, it should cook thirty minutes; if medium, allow thirty-five to forty minutes. Serve with Brown Mushroom Sauce (see [Page 167](#)) using fat in dripping pan.

PARSLEY POTATOES

Wash, pare and cut potatoes in one-half inch cubes; there should be three cups. Blanch by parboiling five minutes in boiling salted water; drain. Melt one-third cup of butter in a frying-pan, add potatoes, and cook over a slow fire until potatoes are soft and delicately browned. Melt two tablespoons Cottolene in a sauce-pan, add a few drops onion juice, one and one-half tablespoons flour, one-half teaspoon salt, one-eighth teaspoon pepper; stir to a smooth paste and pour on slowly one cup hot milk, stirring constantly. Remove from range and add one egg yolk slightly beaten. Pour sauce over potatoes and sprinkle with finely chopped parsley.

BROILED TOMATOES

Select four firm, smooth, ripe tomatoes. Wipe them and cut out the hard center around the stem ends; then cut them in halves crosswise. Rub the cut sides lightly with a clove of garlic and dip cut side in soft butter. Sprinkle with salt, pepper and buttered crumbs, pressing the crumbs into tomato with a broad knife. Arrange them in a well-greased wire broiler and broil with skin side down over glowing coals or under a gas flame until soft, using care that they do not scorch. Remove to hot serving platter, drop a bit of butter on each and serve immediately. Onion juice may be used in place of garlic.

BANANA FRITTERS

3 bananas.
1 cup bread flour.
2 teaspoons baking powder.
¼ teaspoon salt.

1 tablespoon sugar.
¼ cup cream or milk.
1 egg beaten very lightly.
½ tablespoon lemon juice.
½ tablespoon Sherry wine.

PROCESS: Sift dry ingredients together twice. To beaten egg add cream and combine mixtures. Force bananas through a sieve and mix pulp with lemon juice and sherry wine; add to batter, beat thoroughly, and drop by tablespoonfuls into deep, hot Cottolene. Drain, sprinkle with powdered sugar and serve with

ORANGE SAUCE

Make, a syrup by boiling one cup sugar with one-fourth cup water and two shavings of orange rind, four minutes. Remove from range, lift out orange peel, add one-half tablespoon butter and one tablespoon each of orange and lemon juice and Sherry wine.

PEPPER AND ONION SALAD

Plunge a bright-red bell pepper (Ruby King) into boiling water, remove immediately and rub off the outer "shiny" skin. Cover with ice water to chill and become crisp. Cut a slice from the stem end and remove the seeds and veins, then cut in rings as thin as possible. Cut one small Spanish onion in very thin slices, separate the rings and "crisp" in ice water. Drain and toss together both onion and pepper rings. Season with salt, pepper, and pour over two tablespoons oil and one tablespoon vinegar. Crush the pepper and onion into the dressing, then pile it in nests of crisp lettuce heart leaves.

MOCK MINCE PIE

2 Uneeda biscuits, rolled fine.
1½ cups sugar.
1 cup molasses.
¼ cup lemon juice.
2 tablespoons brandy.
1 cup raisins seeded and shredded.
½ cup butter.

2 eggs well beaten.
Cinnamon, Cloves, and Nutmeg.

PROCESS: Mix ingredients in the order given. Add spices to taste. Line a pie pan with Plain Paste, turn in mixture, wet edges and cover with top crust made of Rich Paste; press and flute edges. Bake thirty-five minutes in a moderate oven.

RICH PASTE

1½ cups flour.
⅓ cup Cottolene.
¾ teaspoon salt.
½ teaspoon baking powder.
Ice water.

PROCESS: Mix salt with flour, cut in Cottolene (except one tablespoon) with a knife, moisten with cold water. Turn on a floured board, pat and roll out, spread with tablespoon of Cottolene and dredge lightly with flour, then roll sheet like a jelly roll; divide in two equal parts. Roll out a trifle larger than pie tin.

September
Third Sunday

Menu

Veal, Spanish Style, (In Casserole)

Stuffed Potatoes—Turnips in Cream Sauce

Stewed Corn and Tomatoes

Dressed Endive

Peach Dumplings—Sherry Sauce

Coffee

Cider

VEAL, SPANISH STYLE, (IN CASSEROLE)
 2 pounds veal, cut from leg.
 $1/3$ cup fat salt pork or bacon.
 ¾ cup fine, soft bread crumbs.
 1 teaspoon salt.
 $1/8$ teaspoon black pepper.
 Few grains cayenne.
 1 teaspoon chopped parsley.
 2 cups cooked and strained tomato pulp.
 ½ green pepper finely chopped.
 ½ onion finely chopped.
 1 egg slightly beaten.
 Soda.
 Worcestershire Sauce.

PROCESS: Remove all fat tissue and skin from veal; remove skin from pork. Pass both through meat grinder twice, add crumbs and seasonings, except tomato, onion and green pepper; mix thoroughly and bind together with egg. Shape in balls the size of a small egg. Roll in flour and sauté a rich brown in Cottolene made hot in an iron frying pan. Heat tomato pulp, add one-eighth teaspoon soda, one-half teaspoon salt and one-half tablespoon Worcestershire Sauce. Turn into a warm casserole, add chopped pepper and onion. Dispose balls over sauce, rinse frying pan with a little boiling water or Brown Stock and pour over balls. Cover and let simmer in a moderate oven two hours. Serve from casserole, or arrange on a hot platter and surround with a border of boiled rice sprinkled with finely chopped parsley; place a spray of parsley in each meat ball.

STUFFED POTATOES

Wash six medium-sized, smooth potatoes. Bake, and cut off a lengthwise slice from each; scoop out potato with a spoon using care that the shells are not broken. Pass through ricer, add two tablespoons butter, season with salt and pepper, one-half cup hot milk or cream. Add two egg yolks well beaten, then fold in the stiffly beaten whites. Refill shells with this mixture, using pastry bag and rose tube or pile it lightly with spoon (do not spread smoothly). Bake in a hot oven until potatoes are well puffed and browned.

TURNIPS IN CREAM SAUCE

Wash, pare and cut purple-top turnips in one-fourth inch cubes. Cook in boiling salted water until tender (from forty minutes to one hour). Drain well and reheat in White Sauce using cream in place of milk in sauce. (For Cream Sauce see Page 151.)

STEWED CORN AND TOMATOES

Cut the corn from six ears of tender, sweet, green corn; scrape the cobs with back of knife. Cook until tender in as little water as possible, then add an equal quantity of stewed tomatoes. Add one-third cup butter and one tablespoon sugar. Season with salt and pepper, heat to boiling point and turn into hot serving dish.

DRESSED ENDIVE

Marinate the bleached leaves of crisp endive with French Dressing, adding one and one-half tablespoons finely chopped chives and one-half tablespoon Nasturtium seed cells finely chopped, to the dressing just before pouring over Endive.

PEACH DUMPLINGS

2 cups flour.
4 teaspoons baking powder.
½ teaspoon salt.
1½ cups granulated sugar.
2 tablespoons Cottolene.

⅞ cup cream.
Peaches.
2½ cups cold water.

PROCESS: Mix and sift flour, baking powder and salt; rub in Cottolene with tips of fingers, add cream gradually, cutting it in with a knife. Turn on a floured board, knead slightly, pat and roll out to one-half inch thickness. Shape with a large biscuit cutter. Pare juicy, ripe peaches, cut in halves lengthwise, remove stones, cut in quarters and place three-quarters of a peach on each circle of dough, enclose them, pressing the edges together. Place in a buttered, granite dripping pan one and one-half inches apart, sift sugar around dumplings and pour cold water over sugar. Bake in a hot oven twenty minutes, basting three times. Serve with Hard or

SHERRY SAUCE

3 tablespoons butter.
½ cup sugar.
2 egg yolks well beaten.
¾ cup cream.
3 tablespoons sherry wine.
Few grains salt.
⅛ teaspoon nutmeg.

PROCESS: Cream butter, add sugar, egg yolks, salt and gradually the cream, stirring constantly. Cook over hot water until mixture coats the spoon; add sherry and beat again. Turn in a sauce boat and sprinkle with nutmeg.

Fifty-Two Sunday Dinners

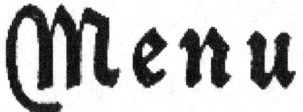

TOMATO SOUP

FRIED CHICKEN—CREAM GRAVY

BAKED POTATOES   CORN FRITTERS

CAULIFLOWER SALAD

PEACH CAKE WITH CREAM

COFFEE

TOMATO SOUP

(For recipe see Page 40.)

FRIED CHICKEN

Dress, clean and disjoint two chickens. Rub chicken over with a half lemon cut in half lengthwise, sprinkle with salt, pepper and dredge with flour. Sauté in hot Cottolene until richly browned, turning often. Reduce heat, cover and let cook slowly until tender. It may be necessary to add a little moisture (about ¼ cup of hot stock or water). Remove to serving platter and surround with Corn Fritters. Pass Cream Gravy.

CREAM GRAVY

¼ cup butter.
1 slice onion.
¼ cup flour.
1½ cups well-seasoned chicken stock.

A Book of Recipes

½ cup hot cream.
½ teaspoon salt.
⅛ teaspoon pepper.

Process: Cook butter in a sauce-pan with onion until onion is delicately browned. Remove onion, add flour mixed with seasonings; stir to a smooth paste and brown lightly. Add hot stock gradually, stirring constantly. Add hot cream and beat until smooth and glossy. The color of this sauce is that of Café au Lait.

CORN FRITTERS

2 cups grated corn.
¼ cup milk.
1⅓ cup flour.
2 teaspoons sugar.
⅓ cup melted butter.
1 teaspoon salt.
⅛ teaspoon pepper.
3 eggs well beaten.

Process: Mix corn, milk, flour, sugar and salt, add eggs. Drop by tablespoonfuls on a hot well-greased griddle and cook as griddle cakes until browned on one side; then turn and brown the other side.

CAULIFLOWER SALAD

Marinate a prepared cauliflower (see recipe on Page 95) with French Dressing, to which add one tablespoon finely chopped chives. Dispose in a nest of peppergrass, water cress, endive or lettuce heart leaves. Sprinkle with grated Edam cheese.

PEACH CAKE WITH SWEETENED CREAM

2 cups flour.
4 teaspoons baking powder.
½ teaspoon salt.
3 tablespoons Cottolene.
¾ cup rich milk.
5 peaches.

Sultana raisins.
Mace and sugar.

Process: Mix and sift the first three ingredients. Rub in Cottolene with tips of fingers, add milk, mixing it in with a knife. This dough must be soft enough to spread in a shallow, well-buttered pan to the depth of one inch. (Add more milk if necessary.) Pare ripe, juicy peaches; cut in halves lengthwise, remove stones and press halves into dough (cut side up) in parallel rows, leaving a little space between rows. Brush peaches over with melted butter, sprinkle with raisins, granulated sugar and lightly with mace. Serve hot with Hard Sauce, or with cream sweetened and flavored with nutmeg.

Oh! You who have been a-fishing
  will endorse me when I say,
That it always is the biggest fish
  you catch that gets away.

—

Eugene Field.

Fifty-Two Sunday Dinners

Menu
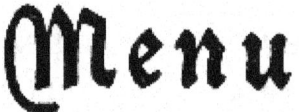

SHRIMP COCKTAILS

POTATO SOUP—CROUTONS

BOILED COD—EGG SAUCE

BOILED POTATOES—SCALLOPED TOMATOES

PICKLED BEETS

STEAMED PEACH PUDDING—VANILLA SAUCE

AFTER-DINNER COFFEE

SHRIMP COCKTAILS

Allow one-fourth cup shrimps broken in pieces for each Cocktail. Season with two tablespoons each tomato catsup, Sherry wine, one tablespoon lemon juice, a few drops Tobasco Sauce, one-fourth teaspoon finely chopped chives and salt to taste. Serve thoroughly chilled in Cocktail glasses.

POTATO SOUP

4 cups potatoes.
1 large purple-top turnip.
3 cups boiling water.
3½ cups scalded milk.
1 onion sliced.
¼ cup butter.

A Book of Recipes

1/3 cup flour.
2 teaspoons salt.
1/8 teaspoon pepper.
½ cup hot cream.
Parsley.

PROCESS: Wash, pare and cut potatoes in one-fourth inch slices. Wash, pare and cut turnip the same. Cover with boiling water and cook ten minutes; drain, add onion and three cups boiling water. Cook until vegetables are tender; drain and reserve water. Rub vegetables through strainer, add water, add milk. Reheat and bind with butter and flour cooked together. Add hot cream and seasonings. Turn into hot tureen and sprinkle with finely chopped parsley.

BOILED FRESH COD

Wash and wipe a four-pound cut of fresh cod. Tie it loosely in a piece of cheese cloth just large enough to cover fish. Place on a trivet in a kettle, cover with boiling water, and add three slices onion, three slices carrot, one spray parsley, a bit of bay leaf, three cloves, a tablespoon salt and one-half cup vinegar. Bring quickly to the boiling point, then reduce heat and simmer gently from twenty to thirty minutes. Hard boiling breaks up the flakes of fish and toughens the fibre. Drain from liquor, place fish on serving platter, remove the skin and pour a few spoonfuls of Egg Sauce over the fish and the remainder around it. Sprinkle finely chopped parsley over all, and garnish with hard-cooked eggs cut to resemble pond lilies.

EGG SAUCE

4 tablespoons butter.
3 tablespoons flour.
1 cup boiling water.
½ cup hot cream.
½ teaspoon salt.
1/8 teaspoon pepper.
4 hard-cooked eggs.
Parsley finely chopped.

PROCESS: Melt one-half the butter in a sauce-pan, add flour mixed with seasonings, pour on slowly hot water, stirring constantly. Boil five minutes, then add remaining butter in small bits. Continue stirring. Add hot cream and two eggs chopped moderately. Garnish with remaining eggs. Pour sauce around fish and sprinkle with parsley.

BOILED POTATOES

Wash, scrub and pare one dozen medium-sized potatoes. If old, let them stand in cold water for several hours before paring, to freshen them. Cover with cold water, heat to boiling point, cover and boil fifteen minutes, then add salt, replace cover and cook until potatoes are soft (about fifteen minutes longer). Drain perfectly dry and shake the potatoes in a current of cold air. Place sauce-pan in a warm place, cover with a crash towel until ready to serve. Serve as soon as possible, if you would have a mealy potato.

SCALLOPED TOMATOES

Season one quart of canned tomatoes with one and a fourth teaspoons salt, one-eighth teaspoon pepper, two tablespoons sugar, one-half tablespoon grated onion and a few grains cayenne. Moisten one and one-half cups of soft bread crumbs with one-half cup melted butter. Butter a deep baking dish, sprinkle with a thick layer of crumbs. Pour in tomato mixture and cover with remaining crumbs. Bake in the oven until cooked throughout and crumbs are browned.

PICKLED BEETS

Prepare beets as for Buttered Beets (see [Page 143](#)). Cut them in slices and lay them in a stone or glass jar. Allow one slice of onion for each beet, one tablespoon grated horseradish, eight cloves and vinegar enough to cover. Let stand twenty-four hours and they will be ready for use. Beets thus prepared will not keep longer than a week. If vinegar is too strong, dilute with one-fourth part cold water.

STEAMED PEACH PUDDING

Fill a two-quart mold two-thirds full of pared, stoned and sliced peaches. Butter the inside edge of mold, also the inside of cover. Cover with a soft dough made by mixing and sifting two cups flour, one-half teaspoon salt and four teaspoons baking powder. Rub one tablespoon Cottolene into flour mixture with tips of fingers, add sufficient rich milk to make a soft dough. Sprinkle peaches with one-half cup sugar, one-fourth teaspoon salt and dot over with one tablespoon butter cut in small bits. Spread soft dough over all, cover closely and steam one hour. Serve at once with

VANILLA SAUCE
1 tablespoon corn-starch.
1 cup sugar.
$\frac{1}{8}$ teaspoon salt.
2 cups boiling water.
1½ teaspoons vanilla.
2 tablespoons butter.

PROCESS: Mix corn-starch, sugar and salt, add water slowly, stirring constantly. Boil gently eight minutes, remove from range, add vanilla, and butter in small bits; stir until well blended.

October
Second Sunday

Fifty-Two Sunday Dinners

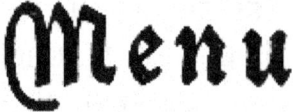

VEGETABLE SOUP

FRIED CHICKEN—BÉCHAMEL SAUCE

BROWNED SWEET POTATOES   STUFFED TOMATOES

KOLE SLAW

BAKED APPLES STUFFED WITH FIGS

COFFEE

VEGETABLE SOUP

½ cup carrot.
½ cup turnip.
½ cup celery.
2 cups potato.
⅓ cup onion.
1½ quarts beef broth.
⅓ cup butter.
½ tablespoon finely chopped parsley.
1½ teaspoons salt.
⅛ teaspoon pepper.

PROCESS: Wash and scrape carrot, cut in tiny cubes; wash and pare turnip, cut same as carrot; wash, scrape and cut celery in thin slices; wash, pare and cut potatoes in one-fourth inch cubes; peel and cut onion in thin slices, mix vegetables, except potatoes, and cook ten minutes in butter, stirring constantly. Add potatoes, cover and cook three or four minutes, add beef broth which was previously strained and all fat removed. Cover and simmer one hour. Put parsley, salt and pepper in bottom of soup tureen and turn in hot soup.

FRIED CHICKEN

Separate two young chickens in pieces for serving; dip in milk, sprinkle with salt, pepper and dredge with flour, or dip in crumbs, egg and crumbs and fry in deep hot Cottolene. Cottolene should not be too hot the latter half of cooking chicken. Drain on brown paper; serve on hot buttered toast with Béchamel Sauce. Double the recipe for Béchamel Sauce (see Page 85.)

BROWNED SWEET POTATOES

Boil sweet potatoes, remove skins and cut lengthwise in one-half inch slices. Cool. Dip each slice in melted butter, sprinkle with salt, pepper and thickly with brown sugar. Lay in a well-greased dripping pan and brown in a hot oven. Dispose around rim of platter containing Fried Chicken.

STUFFED TOMATOES

Select six firm, smooth tomatoes. Cut a thin slice from the blossom end. Carefully scoop out the pulp and mix it with an equal quantity of cooked corn, rice or bread crumbs. Season with salt, pepper, a few grains cayenne, three tablespoons melted butter and a few drops of onion juice. Refill tomato cups, replace the tops, place them in a buttered baking dish and bake thirty minutes.

KOLE SLAW

Shred half a head of cabbage very fine. Soak in cold, acidulated water to cover (add one tablespoon vinegar to one quart water). Drain and mix thoroughly with Cream Dressing. (See Page 50.) Chill and serve in lemon cups arranged in nests of cress or parsley.

BAKED APPLES STUFFED WITH FIGS

Select fine-flavored, tart apples, wipe, core and pare. Fill cavities with washed figs cut in pieces. Bake until tender in a hot oven, basting with hot sugar syrup. Serve cold with thick cream sweetened, and flavored with nutmeg.

SUGAR SYRUP

Cook one cup sugar and one and one-half cups water ten minutes. Add two thin shavings of orange rind to syrup while cooking.

October
Third Sunday

##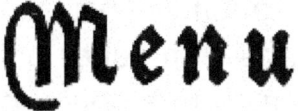

Tomato Soup—Toasted Wafers

Pickles   Celery

Braised Beef—Brown Gravy

Baked Potatoes—Fried Egg Plant

Scalloped Cabbage

Romaine—French Dressing

Cheese Fingers

Peach Duff—Foamy Sauce

Café Noir

TOMATO SOUP

(For recipe see Page 40).

BRAISED BEEF

Select five pounds of beef from the round or rump. Sprinkle with salt, pepper and dredge with flour. Brown richly in a hot frying-pan in some of its own fat; or with fat salt pork tried out, turning often. Place meat in a Dutch oven or an earthen casserole on three thin slices of salt pork, surround with two-thirds cup each of fat salt pork cut in small cubes, carrot, onion and celery, a spray each of parsley, thyme and marjoram. Add two cups Brown Stock or water, the half of a small bay leaf, two small red pepper-pods, or one-half teaspoon pepper-corns, four cloves. Sprinkle all with salt and strew top of meat with cubes of salt pork. Cover closely and cook in a slow oven from four to five hours, basting occasionally. Remove meat and strain the liquor. Rinse the vessel in which meat was browned with stock or water, reserve the liquor. Prepare a Brown Sauce with this liquor following recipe for Plain Brown Sauce (see Page 82).

Serve in a sauce-boat, or turn around meat after placing on hot serving platter. A cup of hot, stewed and strained tomatoes may be added to the sauce, also one and one-half tablespoons of freshly grated horseradish root and one tablespoon of Worcestershire Sauce; all of which improves the flavor.

BAKED POTATOES

Wash and scrub with a vegetable brush eight uniform-sized potatoes. Place in dripping pan, and bake in hot oven forty-five minutes, turning when half done. Take up each potato with a towel and press gently to crack the skins. Put a half teaspoon butter in each potato and serve at once.

FRIED EGG PLANT

Pare a medium-sized egg plant, cut in one-fourth inch slices and soak in cold salt water over night. Drain and cover with cold water one hour, drain again and dry between towels. Sprinkle with salt and pepper, dip in batter and fry in deep, hot Cottolene.

FRITTER BATTER

1 cup bread flour.
½ teaspoon salt.
Few grains white pepper.
$2/3$ cup milk.
2 eggs well beaten.
2 teaspoons olive oil.

PROCESS: Mix and sift flour, salt and pepper; add milk slowly, stirring until batter is smooth; add olive oil and well beaten eggs.

SCALLOPED CABBAGE

Cut one-half large head or one small head boiled cabbage, in pieces. Cover with one cup White Sauce, sprinkle with one-third cup grated cheese, two tablespoons finely chopped pimentos; season with salt, pepper, mix well. Turn into a well-greased baking dish and cover with buttered crumbs; place on grate in oven and bake until heated throughout and crumbs are browned.

ROMAINE WITH FRENCH DRESSING

Remove the wilted leaves from two heads of romaine, trim off the stalk and cut the heads in halves lengthwise (if heads are large, they may be cut in quarters); lay in cold water, cut side down, until crisp. Drain well, dispose on salad plates and pour over French Dressing. Serve two Cheese Fingers with each portion of Salad.

CHEESE FINGERS

Mix one Cream Cheese with an equal quantity of finely chopped English walnut meats; season with salt, black pepper and a few grains cayenne. Moisten with Cream Salad Dressing. Spread between thin slices of white bread and cut in strips the width of fingers.

PEACH DUFF

1 quart thinly sliced peaches.
2 cups sugar.
1 tablespoon Cottolene.
¾ cup milk.
2 cups flour.
4 teaspoons baking powder.
1 teaspoon salt.

PROCESS: Mix and sift flour, baking powder and salt; rub in Cottolene with tips of fingers, add milk gradually, mixing ingredients with a knife. Turn on a slightly floured board, knead slightly, pat and roll to fit top of pudding dish. Butter bottom and sides of dish, put in peaches and sugar in layers. Cover with dough; press edges over edge of dish and steam one hour. Serve in dish in which it was steamed. Serve with

FOAMY SAUCE

½ cup butter.
1 cup powdered sugar.
Yolk 1 egg.
2 tablespoons sherry wine.
Whites 2 eggs.
Nutmeg.

PROCESS: Cream butter; add sugar gradually, stirring constantly, yolk of egg and sherry; continue stirring. Cook over hot water until mixture thinly coats wooden spoon. Remove from range and pour over stiffly beaten whites of eggs. Turn in serving pitcher and sprinkle with nutmeg.

October
Fourth Sunday

Fifty-Two Sunday Dinners

Menu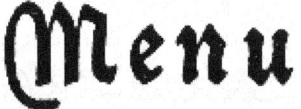

WALNUT AND OLIVE CANAPÉ

CLAM AND TOMATO CONSOMMÉ

BROWNED CRACKERS

SWEET GHERKINS   PICCALILLI

VEAL POT PIE WITH BAKED DUMPLINGS

BUTTERED BEETS BAKED SQUASH

STUFFED TOMATO SALAD

MOCK CHERRY PIE CHEESE

COFFEE CIDER

NUT AND OLIVE CANAPÉ

Cut stale white bread in crescents. Fry a delicate brown in deep hot Cottolene. Drain on brown paper. Mix equal parts of finely chopped olives and English walnuts, season with a few grains cayenne and moisten with Mayonnaise or Boiled Salad Dressing to the consistency to spread. Spread fried bread with mixture and garnish with very thin strips of pimentos; set pimolas in center of each canapé.

CLAM AND TOMATO CONSOMMÉ

To four cups of Consommé add two cups each clam water and tomato pulp. Clear, and add soft part of clams. Heat to boiling point and serve in Bouillon cups.

TO PREPARE CLAMS

Wash and scrub (in several waters) with a stiff vegetable brush two quarts of clams. Place in an agate stew pan, add one-half cup cold water, cover and let simmer until shells open. Remove clams from shells and strain liquor through a napkin. Use only the soft parts of clams.

BROWNED CRACKERS

Spread one dozen Saltines with butter; sprinkle with a few grains cayenne. Brown delicately in a hot oven; serve at once.

PICCALILLI

3 quarts green tomatoes.
2 heads celery.
4 mild red peppers.
2 mild green peppers.
2 large white onions.
2 large ripe cucumbers.
1 cup salt.
1½ quarts cider vinegar.
2 pounds brown sugar.
¼ cup white mustard seed.
1 teaspoon mustard.
1½ teaspoons black pepper.

PROCESS: Chop the vegetables, sprinkle with salt and let stand over night. In the morning drain and press in a coarse crash towel to remove all the acrid juice possible. Add vinegar, sugar and spices and simmer until vegetables are tender and clear. Sterilize fruit jars and fill to overflowing. Seal and store.

VEAL POT PIE WITH BAKED DUMPLINGS

Cut two pounds of veal from the leg in one-inch cubes. Add a fourth-inch thick slice of salt pork, cut in very small cubes. Cover with boiling water. Add one small carrot sliced, one stalk celery broken in pieces, and two slices onion. When half done add one-half tablespoon salt. Cook until meat is tender. Remove the meat and strain the broth; thicken broth with flour diluted with cold water. Put meat into a baking dish and pour over enough of the thickened broth to barely cover the meat. Sprinkle with salt and pepper. Make a soft dough by mixing and sifting one and one-half cups pastry flour, one-half teaspoon salt, two and one-half teaspoons baking powder; rub in three tablespoons Cottolene with tips of fingers, then add milk enough to make a soft dough and drop by tablespoonfuls upon meat—(dumplings should set upon the meat and not sink into gravy) close together to cover the surface. Bake thirty minutes in a hot oven. Serve remaining gravy in a sauce-boat.

BUTTERED BEETS

Wash and scrub beets with a vegetable brush, being careful not to break the skin. Cook in boiling water to cover (about an hour for small young beets, and old beets until tender). Drain and rub off the skins at once; slice, sprinkle with salt and pepper and dot over with bits of butter. Serve hot.

BAKED SQUASH

Cut Hubbard squash in pieces for serving. Remove seeds and stringy portion. Put one-half teaspoon molasses in each portion and sprinkle with salt and pepper. Bake in a hot oven until tender. Put a piece of butter on each portion and serve in the shell.

STUFFED TOMATO SALAD

Select six smooth, ripe tomatoes. Scald quickly and remove skins. Cut a slice from stem ends, scoop out pulp and chill tomato cups. Drain the pulp and add an equal quantity of crisp celery cut in small pieces, cucumber cut in small dice, and shrimp broken in four pieces. Moisten with Mayonnaise Dressing. Refill tomato cups, put a rose of Mayonnaise on top of each, using pastry bag and rose tube. Serve in lettuce heart leaves.

MOCK CHERRY PIE

Mix one and one-half cups cranberries chopped moderately, three-fourths cup seeded and shredded raisins, one cup sugar, one tablespoon flour and a sprinkle of salt. Pile this mixture in a pie pan lined with Plain Paste. Dot over with one tablespoon butter. Add two tablespoons orange juice. Cover with Rich Paste and bake as other pies.

---

*An odor rich
comes stealing,
From out the oven
bright,
That sets my pulse
a-reeling,
And gives my
heart delight.*

R. R.

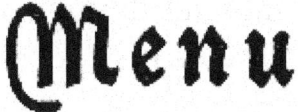

OYSTERS ON THE HALF SHELL

CONSOMMÉ DUCHESS—IMPERIAL STICKS

CUCUMBER PICKLES   CELERY

ROLLED RIB ROAST OF BEEF—BROWN GRAVY

FRANCONIA POTATOES BAKED TOMATOES

SPICED CRAB APPLES

ESCAROLLE SALAD

GRAHAM PLUM PUDDING WITH BROWN SUGAR SAUCE

CHEESE

COFFEE

CONSOMMÉ DUCHESS

(For recipe see Page 15.)

ROLLED RIB ROAST OF BEEF

Have the ribs removed, meat rolled and skewered in shape, from a five-pound rib roast of beef, at the market, (have ribs and trimmings sent with roast). Wipe meat, sprinkle with salt, pepper, dredge with flour and arrange on rack in dripping pan. Place in a hot oven and, when slightly brown, reduce heat and baste every ten minutes for the first half hour with fat in pan, afterwards every fifteen minutes during cooking. (If cooked rare it will require one hour and fifteen minutes.)

BROWN GRAVY

Drain and strain fat in the pan—return three tablespoons to dripping pan, add four and one-half tablespoons flour and brown richly (do not burn flour), add slowly one and one-half cups of Brown Stock or boiling water, stirring constantly. Season with salt, pepper, and one-half teaspoon Kitchen Bouquet.

FRANCONIA POTATOES

Wash and pare six medium-sized potatoes; parboil five minutes. Drain dry. Place on grate around roast beef. Baste with fat in pan when basting roast. Bake from thirty to thirty-five minutes, turning often or when basting roast. Sprinkle with salt and serve surrounding rolled roast, alternating with Stuffed Tomatoes.

BAKED TOMATOES

Select six smooth, firm, ripe tomatoes. Wash, wipe and cut a slice from the stem end; scoop out the seeds and soft pulp. Mix with the pulp an equal amount of corn cut from the cob, one tablespoon finely chopped green pepper, half tablespoon finely chopped onion. Season with salt and pepper, add one and one-half tablespoons melted butter and a teaspoon salt. Mix well and refill tomato cups; sprinkle tops with buttered crumbs. Place tomatoes in a granite dripping pan and bake until tomatoes are soft and crumbs are brown. Remove to serving dish with a broad knife and serve.

SPICED CRAB APPLES

Pick over, wash and drain firm crab apples, do not remove the stems. (Apples must not be too ripe). For eight pounds of fruit allow four pounds of sugar, one quart vinegar, one-fourth cup whole cloves, one-fourth cup stick cinnamon broken in pieces. Boil sugar, vinegar and spices ten minutes. Strain and tie spices loosely in a piece of cheese cloth. Put fruit in strained liquor, also bag of spices, and cook slowly until fruit can be easily pierced with a small wooden skewer (tooth-pick). Remove fruit and fill a sterilized stone jar. Simmer liquor slowly until reduced to half the original quantity; pour over fruit. Lay bag of spices on top; seal and store.

ESCAROLLE SALAD

Marinate the bleached leaves of two heads of escarolle with French Dressing. Chill one hour before serving that it may be crisp. Sprinkle thickly with finely chopped chives and a sweet, red, bell pepper chopped very fine or cut in fine thread-like rings.

GRAHAM PLUM PUDDING

1½ cups Graham flour.
1 cup N. O. molasses.
½ cup milk.
1 cup seeded raisins.
1 teaspoon cinnamon.
¼ teaspoon cloves.
2 eggs well beaten.
½ teaspoon soda.
½ teaspoon salt.
2 tablespoons Cottolene.

PROCESS: Sift flour, spices, salt and soda; add raisins, molasses, milk and eggs, beat thoroughly, then add melted Cottolene. Turn into well-greased brown bread molds and steam four hours. Serve with

BROWN SUGAR SAUCE

5 tablespoons butter.
1 cup soft brown sugar.
½ tablespoon vanilla.
$1/3$ cup thick cream.

PROCESS: Roll sugar, sift and add gradually to cream, stirring constantly. Cream butter and add first mixture slowly, continue stirring. Add vanilla and beat thoroughly with a whip.

Fifty-Two Sunday Dinners

#

Consommé—Bread Sticks

Celery Hearts   Mustard Pickles

Roast Venison   Wine Sauce

Mashed Sweet Potatoes   Creamed Celery

Spiced Peaches

Pepper and Grape Fruit Salad

Mayonnaise Dressing

Nut Bread Sandwiches

Frozen Rice Pudding

Compote Pineapple

Stuffed Dates Salted Nuts

Café Noir

CONSOMMÉ
4 lbs. thickest part of hind beef shin.
1 lb. marrow-bone.
3 lbs. knuckle of veal.
4 cups chicken stock.

A Book of Recipes

Carrot }
Celery } ½ cup each, cut in cubes.
Turnip }
1 medium-sized onion sliced.
3 tablespoons butter.
1 tablespoon salt.
1 teaspoon peppercorns.
½ dozen cloves.
1 small bay leaf.
2 sprays parsley.
3 sprays thyme.
2 sprays marjoram.
4 quarts cold water.

Process: Wipe the meat and bone with a piece of cheese-cloth wrung from cold water. Remove the meat from beef shin and cut it in one-inch cubes. Remove the marrow from bone and brown one-half the meat in the marrow, stirring constantly. Put remaining half in stock pot with cold water, add veal cut in small cubes, browned beef and bones. Let stand thirty-five minutes. Bring slowly to boiling point, skim and let simmer—closely covered—for three hours. Add chicken stock and continue simmering for two hours. Melt butter in frying pan, add the vegetables and cook five minutes, stirring constantly; then add to soup with remaining ingredients. Cook one and one-half hours. Strain, cool, remove fat and clear.

BREAD STICKS

1 cup scalded milk or water.
¼ cup Cottolene.
1 teaspoon salt.
1 tablespoon sugar.
1 yeast cake dissolved in
¼ cup lukewarm water.
White 1 egg well beaten.
3-¾ to 4 cups of flour.

Process: Put butter, salt and sugar in mixing bowl. Add milk. When lukewarm add dissolved yeast cake, white of egg, and flour, reserving one-half cup. Knead until smooth and elastic; cover and set to rise until light, then shape first in small balls, then roll on the board (without flour) with the hands until about seven inches in length, using care that they are of a uniform size, rounding the ends. They should be about the size of a lead pencil. Cover and let rise. Just before putting them in the oven, brush them over lightly with melted butter and sprinkle them with salt. Bake in a slow oven, browning them delicately.

ROAST VENISON

Wipe meat with a piece of cheese-cloth wrung from cold water, spread meat generously with soft Cottolene and sprinkle with salt and pepper. Place on rack in dripping pan, and dredge meat and bottom of pan with flour. Add three slices of onion, six slices of carrot, three stalks of celery cut in inch pieces. Bake one hour in a hot oven, basting every ten minutes for the first half-hour, afterwards occasionally. Serve with the following Wine Sauce. (Mutton may be prepared in same manner).

WINE SAUCE

Put four tablespoons butter in a sauce-pan, brown richly; add five tablespoons flour and continue browning, stirring constantly. Pour on slowly one and one-half cups Brown Stock. Heat to boiling point and add one-third cup Madeira Wine and one-third cup currant jelly previously whipped. When jelly is well blended with sauce, strain and serve piping hot.

MASHED SWEET POTATOES

Wash, pare thinly sweet potatoes, cover with boiling salted water and cook until soft. Press them through potato ricer. There should be two cups. Add four tablespoons butter, salt if necessary, and two tablespoons hot cream or milk. Beat with a slotted spoon until very light. Press again through potato ricer into hot dish.

CREAMED CELERY

Wash, scrape and cut celery in one-half inch pieces; there should be two cups. Cover with boiling salted water and cook until tender. Drain and reheat in one and one-fourth cups of

CREAM SAUCE

2 tablespoons Cottolene.
2½ tablespoons flour.
½ teaspoon salt.
⅛ teaspoon pepper.
1¼ cups hot milk or thin cream.

Process: Melt Cottolene in a sauce pan, add flour, salt and pepper, stir to a smooth paste and pour on slowly hot milk or cream, stirring constantly. Beat with a wire whip until smooth and glossy.

PEPPER AND FRUIT SALAD

Select the desired number of uniform-sized peppers, having half red and half green. Cut a slice from the stem ends, remove the seeds and veins; arrange them on beds of water cress, pepper grass, chicory or lettuce. Fill peppers with the pulp of grapefruit cut in large cubes, Malaga grapes skinned, seeded and cut in halves lengthwise, and butter nut meats broken in pieces, allowing twice the quantity of grapefruit as grapes and one cup of nut meats. Moisten with Mayonnaise Dressing. Fill peppers. Place a rosette of Mayonnaise on top of each pepper, using pastry bag and rose tube. Sprinkle the green peppers with finely chopped green peppers, and the red peppers with chopped red peppers. Garnish top of each with the half of a butternut meat.

NUT BREAD SANDWICHES

1 cup scalded milk.
1 tablespoon Cottolene.
1½ teaspoons salt.
2 tablespoons sugar or molasses.
1 yeast cake dissolved in
¼ cup lukewarm water.
1 cup white flour.
Entire wheat flour.
1 cup pecan meats broken in pieces.

Process: Put Cottolene, salt and sugar (or molasses) in a large mixing bowl and pour on scalded milk; when lukewarm add dissolved yeast cake, white flour, two cups entire wheat flour and nut meats. Mix well and turn on a well-floured board. Add more flour and knead until dough is smooth and elastic. Return to bowl, cover with a cloth; set to rise in a warm place. When more than double its bulk, turn on slightly floured board, knead and shape in a loaf. Place in a well-greased, brick-shaped pan (pan should be half full). Cover, let rise again to top of pan and bake in a moderate oven fifty minutes to one hour. When twenty-four hours old, cut in thin slices, remove crusts, spread one-half the slices generously with cream cheese, cover with remaining slices and cut in triangles.

FROZEN RICE PUDDING WITH COMPOTE OF PINEAPPLE

$\frac{1}{3}$ cup rice well washed.
1 cup cold water.
1½ cups milk.
Yolks 3 eggs.
¾ cup sugar.
2 cups whipping cream.
¼ teaspoon salt.

Process: Add cold water to rice and cook in double boiler thirty minutes. Drain, return to double boiler, add milk and cook until rice is tender, then rub through purée strainer. Beat egg yolks very light, add sugar and salt, then pour slowly on hot rice. Cook until mixture thickens, cool and half freeze. Then fold in the cream, whipped until stiff. Fill a round mould, pack in salt and ice, let stand two or three hours. Drain slices of canned pineapple; add one-half cup sugar to liquor and two shavings orange peel. Place on range and reduce slowly to a thick syrup. Cut slices of pineapples in half crosswise, lay them in syrup for two hours. Unmould pudding and garnish with the pineapple, placing cut side down.

EDITOR'S NOTE:

This menu would also prove very acceptable for a Thanksgiving Day Dinner.

November
Third Sunday

Fifty-Two Sunday Dinners

#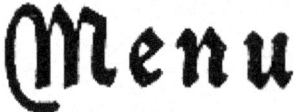

Oyster Soup

Crisp Oyster Crackers

Celery   Pepper Mangoes

Roast Turkey

Bread Stuffing   Giblet Sauce

Cranberry Jelly

Mashed Potatoes—Baked Hubbard Squash

Sweet Corn, New England Style   Creamed Onions

Spiced Pears   Hot Slaw

Thanksgiving Pudding   Drawn Butter Sauce

Pumpkin Pie   Apple Pie

Fruits—Nuts—Raisins—Stuffed Dates

Water Biscuit—Cheese

Café Noir

OYSTER SOUP

A Book of Recipes

(For recipe see Page 162.)

ROAST TURKEY

Select a plump, ten-pound young turkey; dress, clean, stuff and truss in shape; place it on thin slices of fat pork laid in the bottom of dripping pan; rub the entire surface with salt, sprinkle with pepper and dredge with flour. Place in a hot oven and brown delicately. Turn and brown back of turkey; then turn breast side up; continue browning and basting every ten minutes until bird is evenly and richly browned. Add two cups water to fat in pan; continue basting every fifteen minutes until bird is tender, which may be determined by piercing leg with small wooden skewer. It will require from three to three and one-half hours, depending upon the age of the bird. If the turkey is browning too rapidly, cover with a piece of heavy paper well-buttered, placed over turkey buttered side down. Remove the skewer and strings before placing it on serving platter.

GIBLET SAUCE

Drain the liquid from the pan in which the turkey was roasted. Take six tablespoons of the fat, strain the latter through a fine sieve. Return the strained fat to the dripping pan and place on the range. Add seven tablespoons of flour, stir to a smooth paste and brown richly, being careful not to burn the mixture. Then pour on slowly while stirring constantly, three cups of stock (in which the neck, pinions and giblets were cooked). Bring it to the boiling point, and season to taste. Chop the giblets very fine, first removing the tough parts of the gizzard; then reheat them in sauce, and serve.

GRANDMA'S BREAD STUFFING

Remove the crust from two small baker's loaves; slice and pick in small bits; season with one-half teaspoon pepper, two and one-half teaspoons salt, one-half teaspoon powdered sage, and one medium-sized onion finely chopped; mix well, using two forks; melt two-thirds cup of butter in three-fourths cup boiling water; add to first mixture; toss lightly with forks; add two eggs slightly beaten, mix well, and fill well the body and breast of turkey. If bread is very stale, more moisture may be added. If a crumbly stuffing is desired, omit eggs.

CRANBERRY JELLY

Pick over and wash one quart cranberries. Seed two-thirds cup raisins; add to cranberries; add one cup boiling water and boil twenty minutes. Rub through a sieve, and add to pulp two cups sugar and two-thirds cups scalded seeded raisins; cook five minutes, stirring constantly. Turn into a mold previously wet with cold water. Chill and serve.

SWEET CORN NEW ENGLAND STYLE

Chop one can of corn or two cups of green corn fine. Add three eggs slightly beaten, one-half tablespoon sugar, one teaspoon salt, one-eighth teaspoon pepper, one tablespoon melted butter and two cups scalded milk. Turn into a buttered baking dish or into individual ramekins, and bake in a slow oven until solid or custard-like. Serve in baking dish.

CREAMED ONIONS

Remove the skins from one dozen medium-sized onions, under water—to prevent the odor from penetrating the fingers—or grease the fingers before beginning to peel them. Drain, place them in a sauce-pan, and cover with cold water; bring quickly to the boiling-point and boil five minutes. Drain and cover with boiling salted water; let cook uncovered until tender (about one hour), but not broken. Prepare a thin cream sauce made as follows:

CREAM SAUCE

Melt three tablespoons butter in a sauce-pan; add three tablespoons flour; stir to a smooth paste. Add one and one-half cups hot thin cream or milk; season with salt and pepper. Reheat onions in sauce; turn in hot serving-dish, and sprinkle with one-half teaspoon finely chopped parsley.

HOT SLAW

Shave one-half head white cabbage as fine as possible, using a sharp knife. Serve with a dressing made of yolks of two eggs slightly beaten; add one-fourth cup each of hot water and hot vinegar, slowly beating constantly, four tablespoons butter, a few drops onion juice, one-half teaspoon salt, and sift in one-half teaspoon ground mustard and one-eighth teaspoon pepper.

Stir this mixture over hot water until it thickens to the consistency of cream; add to cabbage; mix well; place on range, stirring constantly until mixture is heated throughout. Two tablespoons of sugar may be added.

THANKSGIVING PUDDING

½ cup Cottolene creamed.
1 cup molasses.
1 cup buttermilk.
3 cups flour.
1 teaspoon soda.
1½ teaspoons salt.
1 teaspoon cinnamon.
¼ teaspoon cloves.
½ teaspoon allspice.
½ teaspoon nutmeg.
1½ cups seeded and shredded raisins.
¾ cup currants.
3 tablespoons flour for dredging fruit.

PROCESS: Cream Cottolene. Add molasses and milk. Sift flour, soda, salt and spices together; add gradually to first mixture; beat thoroughly. Mix raisins and currants; dredge them with flour and add to batter; mix well. Turn into a well-buttered tube mold; fill two-thirds full; place on buttered cover; set on trivet; surround with boiling water and steam three hours. Serve with

DRAWN BUTTER SAUCE

$^1/_3$ cup butter.
3 tablespoons flour.
1¼ cups boiling water.
$^1/_3$ teaspoon salt.
½ cup sugar.
¼ cup brandy.
$^1/_8$ teaspoon nutmeg.

PROCESS: Divide the butter into two equal parts. Melt one part in a saucepan; add flour, and stir to a smooth paste; add boiling water slowly, stirring constantly; let come to boiling point. Remove to side of range, and add remaining butter in small bits; continue beating. Then add salt, sugar, brandy and nutmeg. Beat again, and serve very hot.

PUMPKIN PIE

1½ cups steamed and strained pumpkin.
2 tablespoons flour.
1 cup soft brown sugar.
1 tablespoon rose water.
1 tablespoon brandy.
Juice 1 lemon.
Grated rind ½ lemon.
½ teaspoon ginger.
½ teaspoon salt.
¼ teaspoon cinnamon.
2 eggs slightly beaten.
1½ cups milk.

PROCESS: Mix ingredients in the order given. Turn in pie-pan lined with pastry. Bake in a hot oven for the first five minutes to set pastry; then reduce heat and bake slowly twenty-five minutes.

November
Fourth Sunday

Fifty-Two Sunday Dinners

#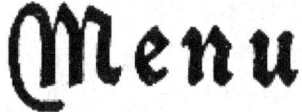

CREAM OF ONION SOUP

CELERY   MIXED PICKLES

STEWED CHICKEN—TEA BISCUIT

MASHED POTATOES

SPICED WATERMELON RIND

NOVEMBER SALAD

SQUASH PIE—WHIPPED CREAM

COFFEE   SWEET CIDER

CREAM OF ONION SOUP

6 medium-sized onions sliced.
1 quart cold water.
1 green pepper chopped.
2 cups scalded milk.
3 tablespoons butter.
4 tablespoons flour.
1 egg yolk.
Parmesan cheese.
Salt and cayenne.

PROCESS: Cook onion and pepper in two tablespoons butter five minutes, without browning; add water and cook until onions are soft (about forty

A Book of Recipes

minutes). Rub through a sieve. Melt remaining butter, add flour and stir to a paste; add gradually scalded milk, stirring constantly. Combine mixtures, add seasonings. Heat to boiling point, remove from range, add yolk of egg slightly beaten. Pass Parmesan cheese and hot, crisp crackers. Two tablespoons cheese may be added to soup when adding egg yolk. Serve very hot.

CHICKEN STEW WITH TEA BISCUIT

Dress, clean and cut up a fowl. Place in stew pan, cover with boiling water. Add three slices onion, one stalk celery broken in pieces, six slices carrot, spray of parsley, one-half teaspoon peppercorns and a small bit bay leaf. Heat to boiling point, skim, cover and simmer slowly until meat is tender; the last hour of cooking add one tablespoon salt. Remove chicken, add one cup thin cream, strain stock and thicken with flour diluted with cold milk or water. Add one-half tablespoon finely chopped parsley. Serve with Tea Biscuit. If a richer sauce is desired, butter may be added to stock.

TEA BISCUIT

2 cups flour.
4 tablespoons Cottolene.
¾ teaspoon salt.
4 teaspoons baking powder.
¾ cup milk.

PROCESS: Mix and sift flour, salt and baking powder, add Cottolene and rub it in lightly with tips of fingers. Add milk and mix to a soft dough with a knife. Toss on a floured board, pat and roll to one-half inch thickness. Shape with a small biscuit cutter, place close in buttered pan and bake 15 minutes in hot oven.

NOVEMBER SALAD

Arrange thin slices of crisp Spanish onion in nests of bleached chicory leaves. Pile on onion Jonathan apples pared and cut in one-half inch cubes, celery hearts cut in small pieces and fresh English walnut meats cut in quarters. There should be an equal quantity of apples and celery, and one cup of nut meats to two cups each of the others. Moisten with Mayonnaise, sprinkle each portion with finely chopped green pepper.

SQUASH PIE

1 cup squash steamed and strained.
1 cup cream or rich milk.
1 cup sugar.
3 eggs slightly beaten.
4 tablespoons brandy or Sherry.
1 teaspoon cinnamon.
1¼ teaspoons nutmeg.
1 teaspoon ginger.
Salt.

PROCESS: Mix the ingredients in the order given, stir until ingredients are well blended. Line a deep, perforated pie pan with Rich Paste; brush over with slightly beaten white of egg. Turn in squash mixture and bake in a moderate oven. Serve cold with whipped cream sweetened and flavored with mace.

"Merry Christmas to friends! Merry Christmas to foes! The world's bright with joy, so Forget all your woes. The earth's full of beauty, of

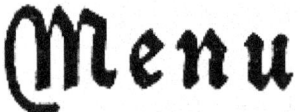

Scotch Potato Soup

Pork Tenderloin Lyonnaise

Baked Apples

Scalloped Potatoes   Fried Egg Plant

Bermuda Salad

Apricot Dumplings—Hard Sauce

Coffee

SCOTCH POTATO SOUP

(For recipe see Page 38.)

PORK TENDERLOIN LYONNAISE

Wipe and split two large pork tenderloins in halves lengthwise; sprinkle with salt, pepper and dredge with flour. Melt two tablespoons each of Cottolene and butter in an iron frying pan, and brown tenderloin richly on both sides in the hot fat. Remove to well-greased dripping pan and add to fat three onions thinly sliced; cook until delicately browned, stirring often. Sprinkle over onions two tablespoons flour, stir well. Put two tablespoons vinegar into one-half cup hot water, add slowly to onions, mix thoroughly. Lay tenderloins over onions, cover closely and cook in the oven until meat is tender. Dispose tenderloin on hot serving platter and pour over contents of frying pan. Vinegar may be omitted and more water added.

BAKED APPLES

Wipe and core eight tart apples; arrange them in a granite dripping pan. Fill cavities with sugar and drop one-fourth teaspoon butter on top of each, sprinkle with cinnamon, sprinkle round one-half cup sugar and pour on one cup cold water. Bake in a slow oven until soft, basting often with syrup in pan. Dispose on serving dish and sprinkle with granulated sugar.

SCALLOPED POTATOES

Wash, pare and slice six medium-sized potatoes. Butter a quart baking dish, lay in a layer of potatoes, sprinkle with salt, pepper, and dot over with bits of butter, dredge with flour and sprinkle lightly with chives. Repeat until potatoes are used and two tablespoons each of butter, flour and chives. Pour over one and one-half cups milk. Cover and bake one hour in the oven. Remove cover and brown top. Serve in baking dish.

BERMUDA SALAD

Slice thinly three or four Bermuda onions. Sprinkle with one tablespoon sugar, one teaspoon salt and cover with ice water. Let stand three hours. Drain and serve with French Dressing.

APRICOT DUMPLINGS

2 cups flour.
½ teaspoon salt.
4 teaspoons baking powder.
1 tablespoon Cottolene.
1 cup thick cream.
Apricots.

PROCESS: Mix and sift flour, salt and baking powder, rub in Cottolene with tips of fingers, add cream, cutting it into flour mixture with a knife. Mix well. Turn on a floured board, knead slightly and roll out to one-half inch thickness. Shape with a large biscuit-cutter and place two halves of peeled apricots (drained from the syrup in the can) on each circle. Enclose them, pressing edges of dough together. Place them in a well-buttered granite dripping pan, one and one-half inches apart; sprinkle round them one cup granulated sugar, pour around two and one-half cups cold water. Bake in a hot oven twenty minutes, basting three times during cooking. Serve with

HARD SAUCE

½ cup butter.
Sherry wine, brandy or vanilla.
1 cup powdered sugar.
Nutmeg.

PROCESS: Cream butter, add sugar slowly, stirring constantly (this gives sauce a fine, smooth grain). Flavor as desired and pass through pastry bag and rose tube onto serving dish. Sprinkle with nutmeg.

December
Second Sunday

Fifty-Two Sunday Dinners

#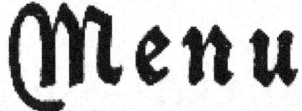

OYSTER SOUP

BOILED LEG OF MUTTON—CAPER SAUCE

SAVORY RICE—STEAMED SQUASH

STUFFED EGG PLANT

LIMA BEAN SALAD

GRAHAM BREAD SANDWICHES

FIG PUDDING

CAFÉ NOIR

OYSTER SOUP

1 quart select oysters.
4 cups scalded milk.
1 stalk celery broken in pieces.
¼ cup butter.
¾ teaspoon salt.
$\tfrac{1}{8}$ teaspoon pepper.

PROCESS: Place oysters in a colander; pour over one cup cold water. Take up each oyster with the fingers to remove bits of shells, reserve the liquor. Heat to boiling point and strain through double cheese cloth, set aside. Scald milk with celery, remove celery and add strained oyster liquor to milk. Plump oysters in their own liquor, take up with a perforated skimmer and lay over butter and seasonings, place in a hot soup tureen. Strain liquor into milk mixture and pour the latter over oysters. Serve at once with crisp, hot oyster crackers.

BOILED LEG OF MUTTON

Wipe meat; pound gently all over with a cleaver. Place in a kettle and cover with cold water, add one small carrot sliced, one turnip sliced, four slices onion, two sprays parsley, a bit of bay leaf and one-half teaspoon peppercorns. Cover and bring quickly to boiling point; boil five minutes. Skim. Reduce heat and simmer until meat is tender (from two to three hours). Add one tablespoon salt the last hour of cooking. Serve with

CAPER SAUCE

3 tablespoons butter.
3 tablespoons flour.
1½ cups strained mutton broth (or hot water).
½ teaspoon salt.
$\frac{1}{8}$ teaspoon pepper.
½ cup capers

PROCESS: Melt butter in a sauce-pan, add flour mixed with seasonings. Stir to a paste and pour on slowly broth in which mutton was boiled, first removing fat. Beat until smooth and glossy, add capers and heat to boiling point. Serve in sauce-boat.

SAVORY RICE

Cook one cup well-washed rice in three quarts of boiling water until partially softened. Drain; add to rice two cups of well-seasoned White Stock; turn into double boiler and steam until rice is soft and stock absorbed. Stir in one-fourth cup butter, one tablespoon finely chopped chives or parsley. Mix well with a fork and turn into hot serving dish. Sprinkle with pepper.

STEAMED SQUASH

Cut a marrow squash in slices, remove the seeds and stringy portions, pare and lay in a steamer. Cook over boiling water until tender. Drain perfectly dry. Mash and season with butter, salt, pepper and a little sugar. Serve hot with tiny dots of butter over top.

STUFFED EGG PLANT

Cut a slice from the stem end of a large egg plant. Remove the inside, leaving a shell one-eighth inch thick. Cut pulp in one-half inch cubes, and cook in boiling salted water until tender; drain. Cook two tablespoons butter with one onion finely chopped, until delicately colored (not brown), add one tablespoon finely chopped parsley. Mix with egg plant, season with salt and pepper, and refill shell. Cover with one-half cup buttered crumbs and bake in the oven until heated throughout and crumbs are brown. Serve in shell.

LIMA BEAN SALAD

2 cups or
1 can lima beans.
French dressing.
Cream Dressing.
2 hard-cooked eggs.
1 tablespoon finely chopped chives.

PROCESS: Cook beans in boiling salted water until tender; drain. If canned French lima beans are used, drain from liquor in can and rinse in cold water. Cover beans with French Dressing, let stand one hour. Drain and sprinkle with chives (onion juice may be used). Mix with Cream Dressing and arrange in nests of lettuce heart leaves. Garnish with eggs cut in quarters lengthwise; dip sharp edge in French Dressing, then in finely chopped chives or parsley.

GRAHAM BREAD SANDWICHES

Rub one cream cheese to a paste, add six olives finely chopped and one-half cup finely chopped pecans. Spread thin slices of graham bread with chive butter. Spread an equal number slices of bread with cheese mixture. Lay one of each together, press edges, trim off crusts and cut diagonally across in triangles.

GRAHAM BREAD

4 cups boiling water.
2 tablespoons sugar.
1 tablespoon salt.
2 tablespoons Cottolene.
1 yeast cake dissolved in
½ cup lukewarm water.
8 cups Graham flour.
6 cups white flour.

Process: Put sugar, salt and Cottolene in large mixing bowl. Pour on boiling water; when lukewarm add dissolved yeast cake. Sift together Graham and white flour, reserving one cup white flour for kneading. Add flour gradually to water mixture, stirring constantly; beat as mixture becomes stiff. Turn on a well-floured board and knead until dough is smooth and elastic. Return dough to bowl, cover and set to rise in a warm place. When dough has doubled its bulk, cut it down with a knife without removing from bowl; cover and set to rise again. When double in bulk, knead slightly, weigh dough and divide into one-pound loaves. Shape loaves, place two loaves in each well-greased, brick-shaped bread pan, brush between loaves with melted Cottolene. (There will be six loaves.) Cover and set to rise; when light, bake one hour in a "bread oven."

CHIVE BUTTER

Cream one-fourth cup butter; add two tablespoons very finely chopped chives. Season with a few grains salt and cayenne.

FIG PUDDING

1 cup chopped washed figs.
$1/3$ cup Cottolene.
3 eggs well beaten.
2½ cups soft bread crumbs.
$1/3$ cup milk.
1 cup soft brown sugar.
1 teaspoon salt.
Grated rind of half an orange.

Menu

Cream of Carrot Soup

Pot Roast of Beef—Mushroom Sauce

Browned Potatoes   Parsley Onions

Parsnip Fritters

Cream Cold Slaw

Steamed Snow Balls—Sauce Soufflé

Coffee—Tea

CREAM OF CARROT SOUP

2 cups chopped carrots.
1 small onion sliced.
2 sprays parsley.
¼ cup washed rice.
2 cups water.
2 cups scalded milk.
½ cup hot cream.
¼ cup butter.
2 tablespoons flour.
Salt, pepper.

Process: Cook carrots in water until tender. Rub through sieve, reserving the liquor. Cook rice in milk in double boiler until soft. Sauté onion a delicate brown in butter, add flour and stir to a paste. Add carrot mixture to milk and pour slowly over flour paste, stirring constantly; heat to boiling point and add cream. Strain into hot soup tureen and sprinkle with finely chopped parsley.

POT ROAST

Wipe five pounds beef cut from top of round; put bits of fat in an iron frying pan, shake over fire until tried out (there should be about one-fourth cup fat). Rub meat over with salt, dredge with flour and sear quickly over in hot fat turned into the pot in which meat is to roast. Add one cup boiling water, cover closely and cook slowly until meat is tender (about four or five hours), turn occasionally, add only sufficient water to prevent meat burning. The last hour of cooking sprinkle well with salt and pepper. Serve with brown gravy made from liquor in pot.

MUSHROOM SAUCE

4 tablespoons butter.
5½ tablespoons flour.
2 cups brown stock.
½ can small mushrooms.
1 egg yolk slightly beaten.
2 teaspoons butter.
½ tablespoon Worcestershire Sauce.
½ teaspoon Kitchen Bouquet.
Salt, pepper.

Process: Brown butter richly (without burning) in a sauce-pan; add flour and continue browning, stirring constantly. Pour on stock slowly, continue stirring until sauce is smooth. Drain mushrooms from the liquor and sauté them delicately in butter. Remove from range, add egg yolk and Worcestershire Sauce; add Brown Sauce slowly, stirring constantly. Reheat over hot water and season with salt, pepper and Kitchen Bouquet.

BROWNED POTATOES

Pare the desired number of medium-sized potatoes; parboil ten minutes in boiling salted water. Drain, dry and place in pan around roast beef, veal or pork, fifty minutes before meat is done. Baste with the liquor in pan and turn often to brown evenly.

PARSLEY ONIONS

Select the desired number of silver skin onions, medium size. Peel and cover with boiling water, bring to boiling point, boil five minutes. Drain and cover again with boiling salted water. Cook until tender, drain and remove to serving dish. Melt one-third cup butter (for one dozen onions) in same sauce-pan, add one teaspoon finely chopped parsley. Pour butter over onions and sprinkle with black pepper.

PARSNIP FRITTERS

Wash and scrub parsnips. Cover with boiling water and cook until tender. Drain, plunge in cold water and rub off skins with the hands. Mash and rub them through a coarse sieve. Season with salt and pepper, moisten with a little cream and butter. Flour the hands and shape mixture in small, flat, oval cakes. Dredge them with flour and sauté a golden brown in melted butter, turning them as griddle cakes. Serve very hot.

CREAM COLD SLAW

Cut a firm, crisp, small head of cabbage in quarters. Cut out the stalk and shave in very thin slices crosswise. Cover with ice water and when crisp drain dry. Mix with the following Cream Dressing. Pile pyramid-like in a glass serving dish, and serve very cold. If cabbage is large, use half a head.

CREAM DRESSING

One cup thick sour cream (not old sour cream). Chill and stir in one teaspoon salt, a few grains cayenne, three tablespoons fine sugar and three tablespoons vinegar, diluted with one tablespoon cold water. Beat well and pour over cabbage, toss lightly with a fork and sprinkle with one teaspoon finely chopped parsley.

STEAMED SNOW BALLS

$1/3$ cup Cottolene.
1 cup fine sugar.
½ cup milk.
2½ cups pastry flour.
3 teaspoons baking powder.

Whites 4 eggs beaten until stiff.
½ teaspoon salt.
½ teaspoon orange extract.

PROCESS: Cream Cottolene, add sugar gradually, stirring constantly. Mix and sift flour, baking powder and salt; add to first mixture alternately with milk. Add extract. Cut and fold in whites of eggs. Fill buttered pop-over cups two-thirds full, place in steamer, cover steamer with a folded crash tea towel, cover closely and steam forty-five minutes. Serve with orange sauce or in nests of Whipped Cream, sweetened and flavored with Vanilla.

EDITORS NOTE:

This will also be found a very acceptable menu for a Christmas Dinner.

December
Fourth Sunday

END

A Book of Recipes

www.ingramcontent.com/pod-product-compliance
Lightning Source LLC
Chambersburg PA
CBHW080021110526
44587CB00021BA/3524